LET'S GET TOGETHER

LET'S GET TOGETHER

Simple Recipes for Gatherings with Friends

by

DeeDee Stovel &
Pam Wakefield

Storey Publishing

*The mission of Storey Publishing is to serve our customers by
publishing practical information that encourages
personal independence in harmony with the environment.*

Edited by Margaret Sutherland and Valerie Cimino
Art direction by Alethea Morrison
Cover design by Sugar and Alethea Morrison
Text design and production by Sugar

Cover photography by John Solem (top left); © Fisher-StockFood Munich/Stockfood (top middle);
Peter LaMastro/Sublime Management (top right); © Michael Paul-StockFood Munich/Stockfood
(bottom left); and © Leigh Beisch Photography/Stockfood (bottom middle and bottom right)

Indexed by Christine R. Lindemer, Boston Road Communications

Printed in the United States by Walsworth Publishing Company
10 9 8 7 6 5 4 3 2 1

Library of Congress Cataloging-in-Publication Data

Stovel, DeeDee.
    Let's get together / DeeDee Stovel and Pam Wakefield.
        p. cm.
    Includes index.
    ISBN 978-1-60342-029-7 (pbk. : alk. paper)
    1. Entertaining. 2. Cookery. 3. Menus. I. Wakefield, Pamela, 1940– II. Title.
TX731.S757 2008
642'.4—dc22
                                        2008005661

Many friends have inspired, advised, contributed, tested, tasted, chopped, blended, and sampled with us. Our children, Wendy and Chip Davis, Meg and Jezz Holland, Liza and Jamie Peck, Kate Stovel, and J.B. and Catherine Wakefield have not only been constructive critics but also enthusiastic and supportive diners. Our grandchildren have been great tasters. We love and thank them all. And to our two Giant fans, Jack and Bill, we are most grateful.

This book is devoted to friendship and the nurturing of friendship through shared meals and times together. It is for those who want to break bread with friends and family and don't mind sharing the preparations with those they care about. II is for those who love good food that is delicious, attractively presented, and nutritious to eat and that doesn't require endless hours of preparation.

Because we learned these things from our moms, we dedicate this book to them:

Beatrice McCoy and **Patricia Clapp**
The Cook and the Writer

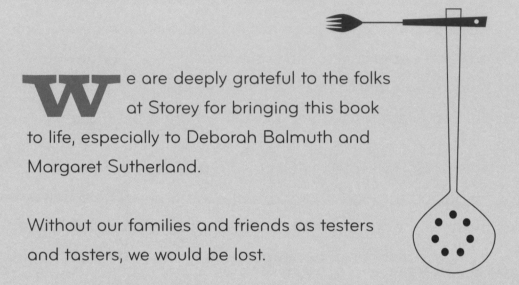

We are deeply grateful to the folks at Storey for bringing this book to life, especially to Deborah Balmuth and Margaret Sutherland.

Without our families and friends as testers and tasters, we would be lost.

CONTENTS

GETTING TOGETHER

We have been good friends for years and have eaten many meals at each other's houses. We both love food that looks as good as it tastes. In writing this book, we realized how different our approaches to cooking are. For DeeDee, cooking is an end in itself. She cooks from scratch, cutting and chopping for relaxation. For Pam, cooking is a means to an end. She has a knack for finding wonderful shortcuts to a great meal and creating a beautiful table. Together we can put on one heck of a meal. We both love to feed people, and here we want to explain how we got where we are, and our different approaches.

DEEDEE'S PHILOSOPHIES AND STRATEGIES

My love of food goes way back, back to the days of my Girl Scout backyard camper badge. After creating "Buddy Burners" of corrugated cardboard set in a tuna can and surrounded by paraffin, and cooktops made from number 10 cans with holes punched on the sides, my friends and I cooked endless little strips of bacon. Squatting around this tiny stove set in my backyard, we watched as the bacon reached the perfect crispy brownness. When we moved into the kitchen, it was to concoct mixtures of brown sugar and butter on the stove, which occasionally resembled pralines and always tasted delicious. My friend Kimmie's mom had a Waring blender *and* ice cream in the freezer. What more could twelve-year-olds want after biking around town all afternoon than a frosty milkshake made by their own hands? "Let's make milkshakes," was the cry that drove us to her house. And, after some instruction from my mom, and many lumps, I became the gravy maker in my family. These experiments were always surrounded by wonderful family meals put on the table by my mom and consumed with gusto by my dad, my brother, my grandmother, and me.

Dinner was a family gathering when my dad came home from his day at work in New York. If there was beef on the weekend, my mom would put together rouladen or porcupines; if it was ham, we had schinken noodles or ham pinwheels. One time my mom strayed from the meat and potatoes theme to make what was unusual for our German-rooted family: a dish made with three cheeses, noodles, and tomato sauce called lasagna. My mom told me never to economize on food, and yet she used every scrap available to put these incredible meals on the table night after night.

And the desserts . . . In the fall there was at least one very large apple pie with a most tender and flaky lumpy-looking crust filled with juicy, sweet apples, touched with cinnamon. In summer, when the neighbors' red currants and raspberries ripened, a luscious, tartly sweet red pudding, rote crütze, appeared, topped with vanilla custard sauce. Frequently we ate mounds of poached egg white sailing across custard in the old-fashioned dessert called floating island, or mountains of meringue resting on tart lemon filling in a lemon meringue pie. On birthdays there was the monstrously high birthday cake with boiled icing. White cake with white icing may not seem so exciting in these days of complex flavors, but when done to perfection, as my mom always did it, it was the absolute best birthday treat.

My skinny dad loved to eat, and my creative mom loved to cook. What better environment for a love of food to flourish?

Depending on who knows what, when I cook I do one of two things. Either I make many recipes at once, use every pot, pan, and bowl in sight, play loud music, and end up with a huge mess in the kitchen as pots bubble on the stove and tempting smells seep out of the oven; or I do what all organized people suggest, which is to create a *mise en place* by prepping everything and putting ingredients neatly into bowls, ready for cooking. Cooking this way makes me feel organized and smug. But the messy way works for me, too. If your time is limited, and everyone's seems to be these days, then I suggest being organized and cleaning up as you go. But if you can't pull that off, don't despair, because if you love cooking and tasting, you will find your own way to do it best.

I tend to make things from scratch and eat them soon after. Once I tried cooking for the week and freezing things because I knew it made sense. Pulling homemade items from the freezer can give great pleasure, too. But then things would get lost in the freezer, and so this method never really caught on for me. However, if apples are in season, I get a bushel of them and make a lot of applesauce and freeze what we can't eat fresh. The same goes for stocks and soups and fresh tomatoes. When having a party, I will make some recipes ahead and try to make my life easier with a few shortcuts, but mostly I work from scratch. Pam is the one who is so good about planning ahead and finding shortcuts without compromise. We always eat well at the Wakefields, and Pam in her effortless way not only serves excellent food but also presents it on an artfully arranged table that is conducive to good conversation.

PAM'S PHILOSOPHIES
AND STRATEGIES

While DeeDee's mom was whipping up rouladen and schinken noodles, my own mom was dreamily shaking Durkee's curry powder over yesterday's leftover leg of lamb. An accomplished writer but a less accomplished cook, my mother (the original multitasker) considered dinner preparation as an opportunity to rethink a troublesome paragraph or reblock Act One. Night after night and year after year, chattering family and a rotation of guests appeared at the dinner table at 6:30 p.m. — not earlier, not later — for a meal that was always nutritious, always well balanced, and usually enjoyable, but rarely inspired. It was my parents-in-law who introduced me to the contemplation and enjoyment of fresh seasonal food prepared with creativity and competence. Lobster Thermidor, veal piccata, and braised endive appeared on the Wakefield table, sometimes at 7:00 p.m., but just as likely at 10:00 p.m. My evolution as a cook was the result of a combination of my mother's systematic countdown to meal delivery and the Wakefields' chaotic inclusion of last-minute guests, and an ongoing discussion of what works best with seviche and how to bone a bluefish.

You should understand that DeeDee is completely at home in the kitchen with a group of any size. She can chat while cooking truly awesome meals. This is a spectacular talent. I need my full concentration to cook, or disasters will result. I can chat and overcook, I can chat and underbeat. I can chat and forget multiple ingredients and key steps, but I can't chat and cook successfully. And so, to minimize anxiety and maximize pleasure, I gravitate to recipes for which a lot of the work can be done in advance. Actually, I like recipes where there is not a lot of work, period. I am more of an assembling kind of cook. I can chat and assemble. My favorite recipes of all are those with interesting ingredients combined in innovative and simple ways. Many of these recipes, collected from talented friends, relatives, local restaurants, and far-flung travels, are included in *Let's Get Together*.

"Presenting" is a major part of entertaining for me. Setting the table and creating a mood are always part of my game plan. I don't use floral centerpieces. I try to avoid competition between the appearance and fragrance of the flowers and the appearance and fragrance of the food. If I use flowers at all, I use just a few, placed in small glass vases or jars and scattered around the table surface. The same principle goes for candles; I like several votives placed around the tabletop so that no one is looking over or around tall candles, and the low diffused lighting is intimate and attractive. I have an assortment of plates, glasses, silverware, and table linens, and I like to mix and match. My mainstay for a large group is the 24 glass plates purchased in my supermarket a few years ago. For casual entertaining and friendly food, I like to use pottery pieces — some patterned, some plain, and sometimes combined with the ubiquitous glass plates. For a more subtle and sophisticated menu, I use old china, again some pieces with patterns and some plain, but all with a similar color palette. I use placemats more often than tablecloths because I like the look of candles and china on polished wood.

I decide on how to serve the food — buffet, family style (passing platters at the table), or pre-plating — depending on the number of guests. Buffet works best for the larger groups, when guests are sitting at more than one table or just using their laps. Family style is good for a congenial and casual gathering. I like to pre-plate food for smaller, more formal meals, when I want each serving to look especially attractive.

DeeDee and I have been inviting guests, planning and preparing meals, and setting tables together for decades. From beginning to end, we enjoy getting together new and old friends over great food.

THE COOK'S PANTRY

A well-stocked cupboard, refrigerator, and freezer will help make all your cooking go smoothly. Having a supply of ingredients on hand makes it easy to cook for guests and spontaneous events. Here's a list of the items we generally keep on hand, many of which are used in the recipes in this book.

IN THE CUPBOARD

- Vegetable cooking spray
- Oils: olive oil for cooking, extra-virgin for dressings and drizzling, canola
- Vinegars: flavored, red wine, white wine, balsamic, and cider
- Kosher and sea salt
- Peppercorns (black and white)
- Herbs and spices (buy small quantities in bulk at a health food store)
- Garlic
- Yellow onions
- Red onions
- Russet potatoes
- Red potatoes
- Chicken broth (canned)
- Plain tomato sauce (canned)
- Italian chopped tomatoes (canned)
- Tomato paste (canned)
- Green chiles (canned)
- Crushed pineapple (canned, packed in juice)
- Mandarin oranges (canned)
- Evaporated skim milk (canned)
- Beans (canned): cannellini, refried, and garbanzo
- Dried beans (assorted kinds)
- Capers
- Sun-dried tomatoes
- Salsa (bottled)
- Good (durum semolina) Italian pasta in a variety of shapes
- Unbleached all-purpose flour
- Wheat germ
- Baking soda and baking powder
- Cream of tartar

- Unsweetened cocoa powder
- Unsweetened baking chocolate
- Chocolate chips
- Dried cranberries, raisins, and currants
- Brown sugar
- Honey

IN THE REFRIGERATOR

- Lemons
- Orange juice
- Mustard: Dijon, coarse-grained, and sweet
- Milk (2 percent, 1 percent, or skim)
- Nonfat plain yogurt
- Cottage cheese
- Parmesan cheese
- Cheddar cheese
- Eggs

IN THE FREEZER

- Basil purée (chop bunches of fresh basil in the food processor, add a little olive oil, and freeze in small containers)
- Chopped fresh cilantro (washed, dried, chopped, and stored in small freezer bags, for soups and fresh salsa all year)
- Gingerroot (can be grated while still frozen)
- Whole cranberries (buy bags when they're in season and freeze)
- Almonds, walnuts, and pecans
- Whole wheat pastry flour
- Tortillas: corn, flour
- Grated mozzarella cheese (grate a chunk and freeze in a bag)
- Boneless, skinless chicken breasts
- Tomato chunks (when in season, wash, cut into 1-inch chunks, and store in freezer containers for fresh tomato sauce throughout the year — much easier than canning or making large batches of tomato sauce to freeze)

BREAK FASTS
& BRUNCHES

FRESH COFFEE IS BREWING, BACON IS SIZZLING, AND FLAVOR-FILLED MUFFINS ARE TURNING GOLD IN THE OVEN.

Breakfast is a wonderful, simple meal. This is the time when company in the kitchen is encouraged. Assign a pair of hands to scramble sunny eggs or flip pancakes. Find someone to pour chilled juice or cut up fresh fruit. Send the less skilled out for newspapers and bagels. Our advice? Keep it simple and enjoy the promise of another day and the warmth and casual chatter of family and friends.

Brunch, on the other hand, generally takes a little more planning. It is a one-event-fits-all entertaining option. It works well for all group sizes and all generations. It can be a joyous part of a wedding weekend or the basis for a festive engagement party, a New Year's Day celebration, or just friends and family gathering. Brunch is a happy choice for the holiday season, when evening entertaining dates tend to get filled early. The traditional brunch menu includes standard breakfast foods such as eggs, pancakes, bacon, ham, pastries, and the like. Our breakfast and brunch recipes offer exciting options. They are fun to prepare and always enjoyed.

So start the plans and the preparation, and "Let's do brunch!"

apple cinnamon stuffed french toast

FLIPPING THIS FRENCH TOAST IS A LITTLE CHALLENGING, but the burst of flavor makes it all worthwhile. The apples can be prepared ahead of time, and the cooked French toast "sandwiches" can be kept warm in a low oven.

4–6 large apples, peeled and sliced	½ cup skim milk
1 teaspoon plus 1 tablespoon butter	¼ teaspoon salt
2 tablespoons sugar	12 slices whole wheat or
1 teaspoon ground cinnamon	oatmeal bread
2 eggs, slightly beaten	Maple syrup and applesauce
1 egg white	

Prep/Cooking Time:
30 minutes

Serves

1   Sauté the apples in the teaspoon of butter in a large skillet over medium heat, until they are slightly soft, about 10 minutes. Mix the sugar and cinnamon in a small bowl and add to the apples. Cook for 1 minute, or until the sugar melts.

2   Whisk the eggs, egg white, milk, and salt together in a deep-dish pie plate until smooth.

3   Dip the slices of bread into the egg mixture; lay six of them out on a work surface. Spread the apple mixture over the bread and cover with the remaining slices to make "sandwiches." Press down slightly.

4   Melt half the remaining tablespoon of butter in a large skillet or griddle over medium heat. When the butter is hot but not brown, add three of the sandwiches and cook until the bottoms are lightly browned. Turn them and lightly cook the other sides.

5   Cook the remaining French toast sandwiches with the remaining butter and serve hot with maple syrup and applesauce.

orange **french** toast

BRIGHTEN YOUR MORNING with the simple additions of orange juice and zest to your French toast. Top it off with orange-infused syrup and you are ready for the day's activities.

4 eggs
4 egg whites
¼ teaspoon salt
1 tablespoon orange zest

½ cup orange juice
1 loaf Swiss Braided Bread
  (page 260), cut into 12 slices

ORANGE SYRUP
1½ cups orange juice
⅓ tablespoon sugar

1 Whisk together the eggs and egg whites in a large glass pie plate. Add the salt, orange zest, and orange juice; mix well.

2 Dip slices of bread in the egg mixture and drain on a rack set over another pie plate.

3 To make the orange syrup, combine the orange juice and sugar in a small saucepan over medium heat. Bring to a boil and cook for 1 minute.

4 Heat a nonstick griddle or large skillet brushed lightly with butter over medium heat. Cook the French toast until browned; keep warm on a serving plate in a 200°F oven until ready to serve. Serve with the warm orange syrup.

Prep/Cooking Time:
30 minutes

Serves

6

overnight **oven** french toast

THE NIGHT-BEFORE ASSEMBLY of this satisfying breakfast or brunch dish decreases morning chaos. And besides that, it will brighten the morning with its simple twist on an old favorite.

2 tablespoons butter

8 slices raisin bread, sliced
  1-inch thick (one 1-pound loaf)

4 eggs

4 egg whites

1 1/2 cups milk

1/4 cup sugar

1/2 teaspoon cinnamon

2 tablespoons maple syrup

1 teaspoon vanilla

1/2 teaspoon salt

  Confectioners' sugar

Preparation Time:
20 minutes

Setting Time:
Overnight

Baking Time:
About 30 minutes

Serves

1 Generously butter a large shallow baking pan and arrange the bread slices in a single layer.

2 Beat together the eggs, egg whites, milk, sugar, cinnamon, syrup, vanilla, and salt in a large bowl. Pour mixture over the bread; turn slices to coat.

3 Cover with plastic wrap and refrigerate overnight.

4 Preheat the oven to 400°F.

5 Bake the French toast for 20 minutes, or until a tester inserted into the center comes out clean. Turn the bread and continue baking until golden, about 4 minutes longer.

6 Transfer the cooked toast to warm plates and sprinkle with confectioners' sugar.

zucchini **sausage** strata

STRATAS ARE PERFECT FOR THE BRUNCH TABLE because they need to be assembled the day before so that the bread can soak up the milk and eggs and puff up for a dramatic presentation. Luscious aromas will fill the house as this soufflé-like concoction bakes. The zucchini, sausage, and sharp cheese combine to provide layers of savory flavors in a rich and satisfying dish.

8 large slices of Italian semolina
    bread or French bread
2 cups grated zucchini
2 sweet Italian turkey sausages,
    browned, crumbled, and well
    drained to remove excess fat
1 medium onion, chopped
2 cups grated sharp cheddar
    cheese (8 ounces)

5 eggs
3 cups low-fat milk
1 teaspoon dried thyme
$1/4$ teaspoon dry mustard
$1/4$ teaspoon salt
$1/4$ teaspoon white pepper
2 tablespoons freshly grated
    Parmesan cheese

1 Lightly coat a shallow 2-quart casserole dish with vegetable cooking spray and line it with four slices of the bread. Scatter the zucchini and sausage over the bread; sprinkle with the onion and cheese. Lay the remaining bread slices over the cheese.

2 Whisk the eggs together in a large bowl until foamy. Add the milk, thyme, mustard, salt, and pepper, and mix well; pour the mixture over the bread. Cover the casserole with plastic wrap and refrigerate overnight.

3 Preheat the oven to 350°F.

4 Sprinkle the strata with the Parmesan and bake for 45 minutes to 1 hour, or until it is puffy and golden brown. Serve hot.

Preparation Time:
30 minutes

Setting Time:
Overnight

Baking Time:
1 hour

Serves

asparagus strata

THIS VARIATION ON THE STRATA THEME IS THE PERFECT DISH for asparagus season, when these green stalks are fresh and lovely. Serve it with a citrus salad and breakfast sausages.

12 ounces sourdough baguette,
    cut into 12 slices
1 pound fresh asparagus, washed,
    ends trimmed, and cut on an
    angle into 1-inch pieces
1 teaspoon lemon zest
2 cups mixed freshly grated
    Parmesan and Asiago cheeses
    (8 ounces)

5 eggs, lightly beaten
3 1/2 cups low-fat milk
2 tablespoons minced shallots
2 teaspoons dried tarragon

Preparation Time:
30 minutes

Setting Time:
Overnight

Baking Time:
1 hour

Serves

8

1 Butter a shallow ovenproof casserole dish. Lay half the bread slices on the bottom of the dish. Spread the asparagus on top of the bread and sprinkle with the lemon zest. Reserve 1/2 cup of the cheese mixture, and sprinkle the rest over the asparagus. Cover with the remaining bread slices.

2 Beat together the eggs, milk, shallots, and tarragon in a large bowl. Pour over the bread, covering all the slices. Press down to be sure the milk mixture soaks into the bread. Sprinkle with the reserved cheese and cover tightly with plastic wrap. Refrigerate for up to 12 hours.

3 Preheat the oven to 350°F. Let the strata sit at room temperature for about 30 minutes.

4 Bake the strata for 45 minutes to 1 hour, or until it is lightly browned on top and puffy. Serve hot.

stewed oranges and apricots

WE WERE FIRST SERVED THIS DELICIOUS CONCOCTION, warmed on a woodstove, at a wonderful old Adirondack mountain camp. A spoonful of this over a steaming bowl of oatmeal topped with cream made us ready to climb any mountain in the high peaks. Try it chilled and served over ice cream, too.

2 oranges, thinly sliced into rounds, then quartered and seeded
1 cup dried apricots, cut into quarters
1½ cups prunes

3 lemon slices
1 cinnamon stick
4 whole cloves
3 cups water
¼ cup sugar

Preparation Time: 1 hour

Makes

2½ cups

Combine the fruits and spices in a large saucepan. Add the water and bring to a boil. Reduce the heat and simmer for 20 minutes, stirring occasionally. Add the sugar and cook for another 10 minutes. Serve warm.

MENU FOR A SIMPLE WEEKEND BREAKFAST WITH GUESTS

- Hot oatmeal with brown sugar
- Stewed Oranges and Apricots
- Assorted juices

- Coffee, tea, and Hot Homemade Cocoa (page 246)

glorious **granola**

THIS IS A WONDERFUL GRANOLA RECIPE. It is high in fiber and has no added refined sugar, but it is just sweet enough. Use old-fashioned oats, not quick-cooking, as their texture seems to survive the baking process well. When packed in glass jars, it makes a welcome gift. Commission your in-house artists to design and decorate labels.

6 cups rolled oats
1 cup wheat germ
1 cup skim milk powder
$^1/_2$ cup sliced almonds
$^1/_2$ cup chopped hazelnuts
$^1/_2$ cup shelled sunflower seeds
$^1/_2$ cup sesame seeds
2 teaspoons ground cinnamon

1 cup honey
1 cup canola oil
2 teaspoons vanilla extract
$^3/_4$ cup golden raisins
$^3/_4$ cup dark raisins
$^1/_2$ cup dried cherries
$^1/_2$ cup dried cranberries

Preparation Time:
30 minutes

Cooking Time:
About 45 minutes

Makes

10

cups

1 Preheat the oven to 325°F.

2 Combine the oats, wheat germ, milk powder, nuts, sunflower and sesame seeds, and cinnamon in a large bowl.

3 Heat the honey and oil in a saucepan until hot but not boiling. Remove the pan from the heat and stir in the vanilla.

4 Pour this mixture over the oat mixture and toss to coat thoroughly. Spread evenly in three 9- by 13-inch baking pans or two roasting pans.

5 Bake for approximately 45 minutes, stirring every 15 minutes, or until the mixture is golden.

6 Allow to cool thoroughly, then mix in the dried fruits. Store in an airtight container at room temperature for up to 1 week or in the freezer for up to 3 months.

creamy scrambled eggs

MY GRANDCHILDREN REALLY LOVE MY SCRAMBLED EGGS. The secret is not so much the addition of the herbs as it is the use of cream cheese. The tiny ones like them served herbless, but when they grow older they love the whole package.

10 eggs	¼ cup chopped fresh basil,
4 egg whites	or 1 teaspoon dried
¼ cup skim milk	¼ cup chopped fresh parsley
1 (8-ounce) package light cream cheese, diced	1 teaspoon dried oregano
	1 teaspoon unsalted butter

1 Whisk the eggs and egg whites together in a large bowl. Beat in the milk, cream cheese, basil, parsley, and oregano.

2 Melt the butter in a skillet over low heat, add the egg mixture, and cook for about 5 minutes, stirring constantly. Serve immediately.

Preparation Time:
20 minutes

Cooking Time:
5 minutes

Serves

MENU FOR A SPRING BRUNCH WITH FRIENDS AND YOUNG CHILDREN

- Creamy Scrambled Eggs
- Wadsworth's Muffins (page 24)
- Apple Sausage Bake (page 18)
- Assorted juices

apple sausage bake

FIRE IN THE FIREPLACE, FROST ON THE WINDOWS, and this fragrant family favorite in the oven. Prepare it the day before serving, then bake it in the morning and serve it alongside eggs and assorted breakfast breads. Savory sausage and tart apples with a dash of sugar combine deliciously in this easy-to-make casserole. Golden Delicious apples are a good choice, but any tart apple will do. This mouthwatering combination has been a welcome part of many breakfasts, brunches, and simple suppers at my house.

Preparation Time:
30 minutes

Baking Time:
45 minutes

Serves
6

1 pound breakfast sausage links, cut in half (use turkey sausage if you find one you like)

6 tart apples, sliced but not peeled

Salt and freshly ground black pepper

1 tablespoon lemon juice

3 tablespoons brown sugar

1 Preheat the oven to 350°F. Coat a 1½-quart casserole dish with vegetable cooking spray.

2 Brown the sausage in a large skillet over medium heat; drain off the grease. Toss the apple and sausage pieces together and put in the casserole dish. Sprinkle with the salt and pepper, lemon juice, and brown sugar.

3 Cover and bake for 45 minutes. Uncover and allow to stand for 10 minutes before serving.

deedee's best waffles

THIS RECIPE EXHIBITS ANOTHER OF THE FINE USES for plain nonfat yogurt in producing light, delectable dishes. These waffles are just plain good! For a crunchy variation, add a half cup of toasted chopped pecans. Serve with pure maple sugar or apple butter, or dust with confectioners' sugar and a scattering of juicy fresh strawberries.

2 egg yolks
$^3/_4$ cup skim milk
2 tablespoons canola oil
1 teaspoon vanilla extract
$^3/_4$ cup plain nonfat yogurt
1 cup all-purpose flour

$^1/_2$ cup whole wheat pastry flour
$^1/_2$ teaspoon salt
2 teaspoons baking powder
$^1/_2$ teaspoon baking soda
3 egg whites
Maple syrup

Preparation Time:
15 minutes

Cooking Time:
About 15 minutes

Makes

small round
waffles

OPTIONAL TOPPINGS
Chopped pecans, chopped apple, wild blueberries

1 Beat the egg yolks in a large bowl. Add the milk, oil, vanilla, and yogurt; mix until frothy.

2 Sift together the flours, salt, baking powder, and baking soda, and add to the milk mixture. Beat until well blended.

3 With an electric mixer and clean beaters, beat the egg whites until stiff peaks form. Stir about a quarter of the egg whites into the batter. Gently fold in the remaining egg whites.

4 Cook on a preheated waffle iron according to manufacturer's directions. Top with warm maple syrup. For variety, have small bowls of chopped pecans, wild blueberries, and chopped apple, to add to the batter before cooking. After spreading batter on the waffle iron, sprinkle a tablespoon of fruit or nuts directly on the batter and cover lightly with additional batter before cooking.

orange whole wheat pancakes

BILL'S CULINARY CLAIM TO FAME is creating and flipping these truly delicious pancakes. Normally, I am not a big pancake fan, but these combine a wonderful light texture with a mellow hint of citrus, and they are irresistible.

1 cup whole wheat flour
1 cup orange juice
1 teaspoon salt
1 teaspoon baking soda

$\frac{1}{2}$ cup vegetable oil
2 eggs plus 2 egg whites, whisked together
Blueberries (optional)

Preparation Time:
15 minutes

Cooking Time:
About 6 minutes

Makes

10
large pancakes

1 Blend together the flour, juice, salt, and baking soda in a medium bowl. Slowly add the vegetable oil, mixing thoroughly. Stir in the egg mixture.

2 Coat a skillet with vegetable cooking spray and heat over medium-high heat. Pour in enough batter for the desired pancake size; sprinkle with blueberries if desired. Lower the heat to medium and cook for 2 to 3 minutes. Turn the pancakes and continue cooking for another 2 to 3 minutes, until golden brown.

OPTION: Skip the blueberries and sprinkle the pancakes with brown sugar and toasted almonds.

meg's scones

MEG SERVES THESE WONDERFULLY LIGHT SCONES to her friends. We love them. Some enjoy them with golden raisins, big fat dark raisins, or tart cranberries. However you make them, don't plan on having leftovers, because they tend to disappear quickly.

2 2/3 cups all-purpose flour
1/2 teaspoon salt
1 tablespoon baking powder
1/2 cup sugar

1/2 cup unsalted butter
1/2 cup currants
2/3 cup skim milk

1 Preheat the oven to 425°F.

2 Combine the dry ingredients in a medium bowl. Cut in the butter with a pastry blender until the mixture resembles coarse crumbs. Add the currants.

3 Add the milk and mix well with a fork. Knead the dough 10 times. Roll into a 1-inch-thick circle and cut into eight wedges. Separate the wedges and bake on an ungreased baking sheet for 12 minutes.

NOTE: Currants are actually dried Zante grapes. Don't use fresh currants.

Preparation Time:
20 minutes

Cooking Time:
12 minutes

Makes

scones

✕ CINNAMON OAT SCONES

Add 1 teaspoon cinnamon, and substitute 1 1/4 cups oats for 1 cup of the all-purpose flour; grind the oats slightly in a food processor before adding.

✕ WHOLE WHEAT SCONES

Vary the flavor by substituting whole wheat pastry flour for 1 cup of the all-purpose flour.

power pancakes

LIGHT AND DELICIOUS! These pancakes are a great way to start the day. The recipe can be easily doubled. To serve everyone at once, arrange the pancakes on an oven-proof platter as they come off the griddle and keep in a 200°F oven until the crowd is assembled. Serve with warm maple syrup. There are other syrup choices, but after having lived in New England for years, I have yet to find a better topping than the sweetness from a maple tree.

Preparation Time:
20 minutes

Cooking Time:
15 minutes

Serves

1 cup all-purpose flour
¼ cup whole wheat pastry flour
¼ cup wheat germ
½ teaspoon baking powder
½ teaspoon baking soda
¼ teaspoon salt
1 tablespoon sugar

1 egg
2 egg whites
1 cup buttermilk
1 tablespoon canola oil
   Butter, maple syrup, yogurt,
      or jam, for serving

1   Mix together the flours, wheat germ, baking powder, baking soda, salt, and sugar in a small bowl.

2   Whisk the eggs and egg whites in a large bowl until they are light and frothy. Pour some of the flour mixture into the eggs and stir well. Add some buttermilk and stir again. Repeat until all the flour and buttermilk are mixed into the eggs. Add the oil and mix again.

3   Place a large lightly greased skillet or griddle over medium heat for a few minutes. Test the temperature by splashing a few drops of water on the surface. If the water "dances," then the skillet is the right temperature for cooking pancakes.

4 Spoon enough batter for one pancake onto the hot griddle. Let each pancake cook for several minutes, until bubbles form on the top and the bottom is golden brown, before turning and browning the other side.

5 Serve with butter, maple syrup, yogurt, jam, or whatever pleases you.

✕ BLUEBERRY PANCAKES

For blueberry pancakes, omit the baking soda, increase the amount of baking powder to 1 teaspoon, substitute skim milk for buttermilk, and add 1 cup blueberries to the batter. You can also use the recipe as is, adding blueberries to each pancake as it cooks, but be forewarned that blueberries react chemically to baking soda, and will give the pancakes a greenish tinge. Baking soda is necessary when using buttermilk, so either alter the recipe or prepare your guests for slightly strange-colored, although fine-tasting, pancakes.

wadsworth's muffins

I MISS WADSWORTH'S BAKERY, which was a Princeton, New Jersey, institution and muffin mecca. Fortunately, I got their muffin secrets before they closed their doors. The following were among those most requested by sleepy students and class-bound faculty.

1 ¾ cups all-purpose flour (replace
    ¹/₂ cup with whole wheat pastry
    flour if desired)
¹/₂ cup sugar
1 tablespoon baking powder
¹/₂ teaspoon salt
    Spices (add according to recipe
    variations)
1 egg

¾ cup vegetable oil, or ¹/₂ cup
    oil and ¹/₃ cup applesauce
¹/₂ cup skim milk
¹/₂ cup plain nonfat yogurt
¹/₂ teaspoon vanilla extract
    Additions (see next page
    for recipe variations)

Preparation Time:
20 minutes

Baking Time:
20–30 minutes

Makes

medium muffins

1 Preheat the oven to 400°F. Coat the inside of muffin pans with vegetable cooking spray.

2 Sift the flour, sugar, baking powder, salt, and spices together into a large bowl.

3 Beat together the egg, oil, milk, yogurt, and vanilla in a medium bowl. Pour the wet ingredients into the dry mixture, stirring until the ingredients are just barely combined. Do not overmix.

4 Gently fold in any additions for the selected variation. Distribute them evenly throughout the batter with as few strokes as possible.

5 Immediately spoon the batter into the muffin pans. Bake for 20 to 30 minutes, or until a tester inserted into the center of the muffin comes out clean. (Baking time will vary greatly depending on the variation.) Rotate the muffin pans 180 degrees halfway through the baking process.

✕ RASPBERRY HAZELNUT

1 cup fresh or frozen raspberries
¹/₂ teaspoon ground cinnamon
   mixed with 2 tablespoons sugar
¹/₂ cup toasted chopped hazelnuts

Add the raspberries to the batter. Top the muffins with cinnamon-sugar and chopped hazelnuts before baking.

✕ APPLE WALNUT

¹/₂ teaspoon ground cinnamon
¹/₄ teaspoon ground nutmeg
1 ¹/₃ cups peeled and diced apples
¹/₂ cup chopped walnuts

Add all the ingredients except 2 tablespoons of the walnuts to the batter. Finely chop the reserved walnuts and sprinkle them on top before baking.

✕ BLUEBERRY CRUMB

1 cup fresh or frozen blueberries
¹/₂ cup flour
¹/₂ cup sugar
   Pinch of salt
4 tablespoons unsalted butter

Add the blueberries to the batter. Rub together the flour, sugar, salt, and butter to resemble coarse crumbs, and top the muffins with the mixture before baking.

✕ LEMON POPPY

2 tablespoons poppy seeds
   Zest of 1 lemon

Add both ingredients to the batter.

✕ BANANA BRAN

¹/₂ cup unprocessed bran
1 cup mashed banana

Add the bran to the dry ingredients in step 2. Add the banana to the wet ingredients in step 3.

big breakfast **popover**

THIS IS A CROSS BETWEEN A BIG POPOVER and an oven pancake. It makes a spectacular appearance and is very easy to put together. The pan you use is important. If you have a paella pan or a large, shallow, attractive casserole dish, use it. I have relied on my old faithful Pyrex baking dish. Just don't choose a deep-sided dish. Determine the capacity of your pan with premeasured cups of water before you start filling it. It must hold 3 to 4 quarts.

Preparation Time:
15 minutes

Baking Time:
20 minutes

Serves

5 tablespoons unsalted butter
4 eggs
1 cup skim milk

1 cup whole wheat pastry or
    all-purpose flour (or a
    combination of the two)
1 ¼ teaspoons ground cinnamon

1 Preheat the oven to 425°F.

2 Put the butter in a 3- to 4-quart casserole dish and place in the hot oven to melt.

3 Beat the eggs at high speed in a medium bowl. Reduce the speed and slowly add the milk, and then the flour and cinnamon. Beat until thoroughly mixed.

4 Remove the pan from the oven and pour in the batter. Bake for about 20 minutes, or until puffed and golden brown. Cut in wedges and serve immediately on warm plates with toppings of your choice.

OPTIONAL TOPPINGS:
- Confectioners' sugar with a spritz of lemon juice
- Warm maple syrup
- Sliced seasonal fruit

popovers

POPOVERS MUST BE EATEN while they are hot. Happily, they can be made ahead, frozen, and reheated for serving on the weekend. For best results, though, I recommend them fresh from the oven. Place in a napkin-lined basket and serve with unsalted butter and wonderful jams and jellies. Poke a hole in the bottom of the popover and slide a pat of butter into the steaming interior. When it melts, break the popover apart and add some jelly. This recipe has been tested by thousands of seventh graders in cooking classes with hardly a failure. For many it became a family favorite.

1 cup all-purpose flour

¼ teaspoon salt

1 cup milk

2 tablespoons canola oil

2 eggs

1 Preheat the oven to 450°F. Spray a muffin or popover pan with vegetable cooking spray. Use good-quality nonstick pans to avoid the tragedy of "stuck" popovers.

2 Mix the flour and salt together in a large bowl. In another bowl, beat together the milk, oil, and eggs. Add the milk mixture to the flour and whisk until the batter is smooth.

3 Pour the batter evenly into the muffin pan. Bake for 15 minutes. Turn the oven down to 350°F and bake for another 15 minutes. Remove popovers from the pan and enjoy them while they're *hot*.

Preparation Time:
15 minutes

Baking Time:
30 minutes

Makes

12

popovers

STARTERS AND SMALL PLATES

APPETIZERS FILL THE GAP AFTER GUESTS ARRIVE AND BEFORE DINNER IS SERVED.

he goal is to whet the appetite rather than to destroy it. Getting the balance just right can be a challenge. If you are offering a substantial main course, choose something light to start. Flavorful appetizers work with a mildly flavored entrée, and something crunchy is an excellent choice when soup or stew is the main dish.

Small plates can also be part of a "grazing" meal on their own. Serving tasting portions is an exciting way to entertain without the formalities of three courses and a table to set. The serving size is crucial; make it just large enough to provide a significant taste.

For each grazer, think about teacup-size servings of soup, perhaps one or two plump caramelized scallops, a sliver of Brie and Pear Pizza (page 44), delicate mushroom puffs, a tiny plate of Italian Bean Salad (page 66), two to three small slices of Tuscan Pork Tenderloin (page 145), a shot-glass serving of Mousse au Chocolat (page 223), and a choice of Light Lemon Bars (page 234) or mini Super Chip Cookies (page 226). The possibilities are limitless, so use your imagination, and mix and match our recipes from this and every other section of the book.

crudités with salsa verde

IF "EATING THE RAINBOW" IS OUR NUTRITIONAL AIM, this combination scores an A+. It is easy, beautiful, and healthy. Keep a jar of this glossy deep green salsa in the refrigerator for covert between-meal dipping.

SALSA VERDE

2 scallions, chopped
1 garlic clove, chopped
$\frac{1}{2}$ cup chopped fresh parsley
3 anchovy fillets, drained

$\frac{1}{3}$ cup lemon juice
$\frac{1}{3}$ cup extra-virgin olive oil
2 tablespoons capers, drained

Kale leaves for garnish
Crudités of your choice

Preparation Time:
10 minutes

Serves

4–6

1 Combine all the salsa ingredients except the capers in a blender or food processor with a metal blade. Process until well blended. Stir in the capers and transfer to a serving bowl.

2 Cover a large glass plate with kale, and arrange the crudités in an attractive, colorful circle, leaving space in the center for the bowl of Salsa Verde.

CRUDITÉS SUGGESTIONS ✕

- Small white mushroom caps
- Red bell pepper slices
- Green bell pepper slices
- Yellow bell pepper slices
- Cauliflower florets
- Broccoli florets
- Baby carrots
- Snow peas
- Zucchini slices

spinach dip

THIS HEALTHY, FAMILIAR DIP can easily be doubled to feed a crowd. Savory and colorful, with a creamy texture, it is perfect with crisp cut-up vegetables or crunchy crackers.

1 (10-ounce) package frozen chopped spinach, thawed and squeezed dry

1/4 cup well-mixed dried vegetable soup mix

1/2 cup plain nonfat yogurt

3 tablespoons light mayonnaise

1/2 cup sour cream

1/2 cup canned water chestnuts, drained and chopped

1/2 cup chopped chives or scallions

Combine all the ingredients in a medium bowl and mix well. Chill and serve.

NOTE: If you would like a lighter version of this recipe, try it with the Mock Sour Cream recipe that follows.

Preparation Time: 20 minutes

Chilling Time: 2 hours

Makes

cups

MOCK SOUR CREAM

Makes 1 cup
- 1 cup low-fat cottage cheese
- 2 tablespoons buttermilk
- 1/2 to 1 teaspoon lemon juice

Combine all ingredients in a blender and blend until smooth, scraping the sides of the container often with a rubber spatula.

chips and dip

THIS TRIO OF DIPS is a perfect complement to tacos or nachos. On their own they will enhance any type of corn chip, including my favorite, chile lime. Black beans cooked with bacon make a most satisfying statement, blue cheese and yogurt added to avocado give you a guacamole with attitude, and Kate's salsa sparkles with fresh flavors.

✕ BLACK BEAN DIP

Preparation Time:
20 minutes

Cooking Time:
1 1/2 hours

Makes

2 1/2

cups

2 cups dried black beans
1 1/2 quarts water
1 thin slice salt pork or bacon
3 fresh cilantro sprigs, plus
    more as desired
1 bay leaf
4 garlic cloves, crushed
1 jalapeño pepper, seeded
  Salt and freshly ground
    black pepper
1 tomato, chopped and seeded
2 tablespoons chopped
    fresh cilantro

1 Combine the first seven ingredients in a large pot and bring to a boil. Reduce the heat and simmer, partially covered, for 1 1/2 hours, or until the beans are tender. Add more water as needed to cover.

2 Remove the salt pork and bay leaf. Mash the beans with a potato masher or process half of them in a food processor. Combine all the beans in a bowl and season with salt and pepper and additional cilantro, if desired. The beans may be refrigerated or frozen at this point.

3 Add the tomato and chopped cilantro when ready to serve. You will have a textured mixture with some whole beans and some mashed ones.

✕ BLUE CHEESE AVOCADO DIP

1 large ripe avocado
1–2 tablespoons lime juice
¼ cup crumbled blue cheese
2 tablespoons nonfat plain yogurt
¼ teaspoon salt
Dash of hot sauce
Freshly ground black pepper
1 Roma tomato, chopped
(optional)

Cut the avocado in half, remove the pit, and scoop out the flesh with a spoon. Place in a medium bowl and mash with a fork. Add the remaining ingredients, taste, and adjust the flavors to your liking.

Preparation Time: 10 minutes

Makes

1

cup

✕ KATE'S FRESH SALSA

2 large tomatoes, chopped
and seeded
1 medium Vidalia or sweet onion,
chopped
2 tablespoons lime juice
⅓ cup chopped fresh cilantro
2 tablespoons chopped canned
green chiles
2 drops of Tabasco sauce
Salt and freshly ground
black pepper

Mix all the ingredients in a medium bowl. Let stand for 30 minutes to blend the flavors. If you make the salsa ahead of time, leave out the chiles and add just before serving.

Preparation Time: 15 minutes

Makes

cups

wedding cake cheese

THIS IS YOUR CHOICE FOR AN INCREDIBLY SIMPLE APPETIZER with a lot of visual appeal. You can vary the types of cheese, but they must be round to give the "wedding cake" effect. For edible flowers you may use violets, nasturtiums, pansies, or, for a spectacular presentation, roses. Just be sure the flowers are unsprayed.

Preparation Time:
15–30 minutes

Makes

20
small
servings

3 round, soft cheeses of
  3 different sizes, such as Brie,
  Camembert, and Saga Blue

Fresh edible flowers
Toast triangles and assorted
  crackers

Arrange the cheeses on a doily on a plate in descending sizes, like a tiered wedding cake. Decorate with fresh flowers. Serve at room temperature with toast triangles and plain crackers.

yogurt spread

YOGURT CHEESE CONCENTRATES THE TANGINESS OF YOGURT into a more solid mass, which can then be flavored and spread. You can make it a day or two ahead; refrigerate after making it. Serve this spread on crackers accompanied by slivers of smoked salmon.

Preparation Time:
10 minutes

Chilling Time:
Overnight

Makes

1
cup

³/₄ cup yogurt cheese (1 ¹/₂ cups
  nonfat plain yogurt, strained
  through cheesecloth overnight
  to remove liquid)

¹/₄ cup light mayonnaise
1 tablespoon minced fresh dill
1 tablespoon lemon juice

Mix all the ingredients together in a small bowl and chill.

pesto torte

THOUGH SOMEWHAT LABOR INTENSIVE, this appetizer is always greeted with rave reviews and is one of my favorites to eat and serve. Tomatoes and basil in any form are unbeatable, and the color, flavor, and texture here are sensational. For a holiday or other special event, this creamy savory delight is well worth the effort.

18 ounces goat cheese, softened
$\frac{1}{2}$ cup basil pesto
12 ounces light cream cheese, softened
$\frac{1}{4}$ cup crumbled feta cheese

$\frac{1}{2}$ cup sliced oil-packed sun-dried tomatoes, well drained
Assorted plain crackers, such as water biscuits

1 Shape the goat cheese into a 1-inch high circle with a flat top on a large round serving plate. Spread with a layer of pesto about $\frac{1}{8}$-inch thick.

2 Mix the cream cheese and feta together and shape into a smaller circle on top of the pesto layer. Cover with plastic wrap and refrigerate until ready to serve.

3 Spread most of the sun-dried tomatoes on the cream cheese layer. Sprinkle the remaining tomatoes over the entire creation, allowing some to fall on the first tier and sides. Arrange the crackers around the cheeses and serve at room temperature.

Preparation Time:
15–30 minutes

Makes

20

small
servings

little dogs with currant mustard sauce

THESE DOGS ARE DEFINITELY NOT in the low-fat category, but we always have them at our Christmas brunch. They disappear quickly and couldn't be simpler to make.

1 pound miniature kielbasa
   (Polish smoked sausage)
   or cocktail-size hot dogs,
   or a combination
2 tablespoons Dijon mustard,
   plus more for serving
$\frac{1}{2}$ cup currant jelly
   Horseradish (optional)

Prep/Cooking Time:
20 minutes

Serves

8–12

1 Preheat the oven to 350°F.

2 Place the sausages on a baking sheet and roast them for 15 minutes, or until they are slightly browned.

3 Mix the mustard and jelly in a chafing dish; heat in the oven until the jelly melts and the mixture is smooth. Add the sausages and keep warm. Serve in the chafing dish with toothpicks, more mustard, and/or horseradish, if desired.

smoked **bluefish** spread

I FIRST HAD A VERSION OF THIS SPREAD ON NANTUCKET and spent the following several months trying to track down or re-create the recipe. At first glance, you may find the list of ingredients uninspiring, but trust me and try it. It was worth all my detective work.

1 pound smoked bluefish fillet
6 ounces light cream cheese, softened
1 tablespoon butter, softened
2 teaspoons prepared horseradish

1 tablespoon minced red onion, plus more for garnish
2 teaspoons Dijon mustard
Dash of Tabasco sauce
Salt and freshly ground black pepper

1 Remove the skin and any remaining bones from the fish. Trim the dark portion of the flesh from the skin side of the fish and discard.

2 Cut the fish into cubes and add to a food processor bowl along with all the other ingredients except for the salt, pepper, and garnish. Using the metal blade, process until you have a smooth purée. Season to taste with salt and pepper.

3 Scoop into a brightly colored bowl and garnish with minced red onion.

Preparation Time: 20 minutes

Serves

gravlax with mustard dill sauce

I ONCE SERVED GRAVLAX at a dinner party with a Swedish theme. My next gravlax experience was in Stockholm, when our Swedish friend Binge served it to us with Swedish mustard. We loved it! Gravlax is simple to make — the secret is getting very fresh salmon.

3 pounds salmon fillets, cut in
   half lengthwise
1 large bunch fresh dill
1/4 cup coarse salt

1/4 cup sugar
Crushed white or black
   peppercorns
Thin rye crackers or rye bread

MUSTARD DILL SAUCE

4 tablespoons dark, spicy mustard
1 teaspoon dry mustard
3 tablespoons sugar

3 tablespoons white vinegar
1/4 cup canola oil
3 tablespoons chopped fresh dill

Preparation Time:
25 minutes

Marinating Time:
Several days

Serves

8–10

1 Rinse the fillets and pat dry; lay half of the fillet pieces, skin side down, in a glass or enameled baking dish. Spread a layer of dill over the salmon and sprinkle with the salt, sugar, and peppercorns. Top with the other half of the salmon, skin side up, and cover lightly with plastic wrap.

2 Place a cutting board on top of the salmon and load heavy objects onto the board. Marinate the salmon for 2 to 3 days in the refrigerator, turning several times. The salmon will compact slightly from the weight.

3 Make the sauce shortly before you serve the gravlax. Whisk together the mustard, dry mustard, sugar, and vinegar in a small bowl. Slowly drizzle in the oil, whisking all the time, until the sauce is thick. Stir in the dill.

4 When ready to serve, scrape off the marinade and thinly slice the gravlax on the diagonal. Serve with the sauce on rye crackers or bread.

hot crab dip

HORSERADISH ADDS A SUBTLE ZIP to this creamy, addictive favorite. I have tried many crab dips over the years, and this one simply tastes best. Prep it a day ahead and keep it chilled. Remove the dip from the refrigerator 30 minutes before you are ready to bake, serve, and enjoy it.

1 (8-ounce) package cream
cheese, softened with
1 tablespoon milk
1 (7½-ounce) can crab meat,
drained and flaked
2 tablespoons finely
chopped onion
2 teaspoons cream-style
horseradish

¼ teaspoon salt
¼ teaspoon freshly ground pepper
(white if possible)
¼ cup slivered almonds,
lightly toasted
Crostini

Preparation Time:
15 minutes

Baking Time:
15 minutes

Serves
6

Preheat the oven to 350°F. Combine all the ingredients in a small oven-proof dish suitable for serving. Sprinkle with the slivered almonds. Bake for 15 minutes. Serve hot.

après-ski snacks

THESE SNACKS GO WAY BACK to my early skiing days. Once at a lodge in Vermont, these appeared by the fireside with hot buttered rum. They're so simple to make and incredibly flavorful that they have become a favorite appetizer on cold winter days, especially after a day on the slopes or cross-country skiing through the woods.

10 slices sturdy whole-grain bread
$\frac{1}{3}$ cup light mayonnaise
$\frac{1}{3}$ cup nonfat plain yogurt
2 tablespoons light sour cream

1 medium onion, finely chopped
$\frac{1}{4}$ cup freshly grated
Parmesan cheese

Prep/Baking Time:
15 minutes

Makes

small
servings

1 Preheat the broiler. Arrange the bread slices on a large baking sheet.

2 Mix together the mayonnaise, yogurt, sour cream, and onion; spread about 2 tablespoons on each bread slice. Sprinkle with the cheese and cut each piece of bread into quarters.

3 Broil 6 inches from the heat for a few minutes, until the tops are lightly browned. Arrange on a platter and pass around to the hungry crowd.

NOTE: This recipe can easily be multiplied.

CHEESE FLIGHTS

A cheese flight is a collection of complementary but contrasting cheeses served together. You might choose to go all French, all Italian, or all American. You might choose all cheddar. You might choose all semi-soft. In general, you want to progress from a more mild cheese to a stronger-tasting cheese.

To compose the plate, make sure the cheeses are at room temperature, and label each one. Serve them in wedges, either on a large board, a platter, or a marble slab, but don't let the cheeses touch each other. Or use a mixture of individual plates and small boards. Be sure that each cheese has its own knife or spreader. Provide small plates for the guests. If this is to be the main meal, figure 4 ounces per person. If the cheese is to be served before or after dinner, figure 2 ounces per person. Here are some suggestions to get you started:

SEMI-SOFT FLIGHT
Camembert, Havarti, and Brie.

ITALIAN FLIGHT
Gorgonzola, provolone, and Grana Padano.

FRENCH FLIGHT
Roquefort, Caprice des Dieux, Montrachet, and French Emmental.

CHEDDAR FLIGHT
Aged white, medium yellow, smoked cheddar, and cheddar layered with blue cheese.

Serve cheese flights with sliced apples or pears, grapes, figs, dried fruits, walnuts, toasted pine nuts or pistachios, wheat crackers, and/or toasted baguette slices.

Traditionally, red wines have been served with cheese, but now anything goes, so look for a balance of flavors in which neither wine nor cheese dominates. You might also offer sparkling or still apple cider.

healthy nachos

NACHOS, A FAVORITE SNACK WITH ENDLESS VARIATIONS, are fun and easy to make. Use your imagination to create your own version. Some have sliced black olives; others have jalapeños or guacamole. Monterey Jack is a standard, but there is no reason you can't use cheddar. You could use store-bought tortilla chips for your nachos, but these baked chips are low in fat, delicious, and simple. Put the young teenagers to work on them.

12 corn tortillas (the thinner
    the better)
2 teaspoons butter, melted
1/2 cup refried beans or cooked
    black beans

1 cup grated low-fat Monterey
    Jack cheese or other cheese
    that melts well (4 ounces)
Toppings of your choice,
    such as olives, jalapeños,
    guacamole, salsa, etc.

Preparation Time:
30 minutes

Serves
8

1 To make the baked corn chips, preheat the oven to 350°F.

2 Brush the tortillas with the butter and cut into 8 pie-shaped wedges using kitchen shears. Arrange the wedges in a single layer on a cookie sheet; bake for about 10 minutes, or until crisp and slightly brown. Store in an airtight container for up to 1 week.

3 To finish the nachos, spread some of the chips in a 10-inch deep-dish pie plate. Dab each with refried beans. Sprinkle the cheese over the top. Microwave for 30 seconds on High.

4 Top with any combination of the toppings.

TIP FOR APPETIZER: Make one nacho plate with beans and one without. Put the toppings in small bowls, give each person a small plate, and let people build their own nachos.

asian **torte**

THE JAPANESE WORD FOR "DELICIOUS FLAVOR" IS *UMAMI*. Umami is the fifth element of taste, an indescribable savory earthiness that you can taste as readily as sweet, sour, salty, and bitter. Soy sauce is rich in umami. When combined with the mild flavor and smooth creamy texture of the cheese, the heat of the wasabi, the crunch of the sesame seeds, and the fresh crisp taste of the scallions, the result is this surprisingly delicious flavor-packed spread. After you have tried this recipe, you may want to adjust the amounts of wasabi and soy sauce to suit your own taste.

1 (8-ounce) package Neufchâtel or low-fat cream cheese

4 teaspoons hot wasabi squeeze (usually found in the supermarket's mustard section)

2 tablespoons low-sodium soy sauce

3–4 thinly sliced scallions (white and green parts), about ½ cup

1 teaspoon black sesame seeds

Rice crackers

1 Slice the cheese in half lengthwise into two flat layers. Place one layer of cheese on a small platter.

2 Drizzle 2 teaspoons of the wasabi squeeze over the cheese. Drizzle 1 tablespoon of the soy sauce over the wasabi squeeze. Scatter ¼ cup of the scallions over the wasabi-soy mixture. Sprinkle ½ teaspoon of the sesame seeds over the scallions.

3 Carefully lay the remaining cheese layer on top and repeat the layers using the remaining 2 teaspoons wasabi squeeze, 1 tablespoon soy sauce, ¼ cup scallions, and ½ teaspoon sesame seeds.

4 Serve with rice crackers.

Preparation Time: 10 minutes

Serves

brie and pear pizza

AS AN INVETERATE PIZZA LOVER, I am always on the lookout for wonderful thin-crusted pizzas. This unusual one, originally made at the Store at Five Corners in Williamstown, Massachusetts, is one of my favorites for lunch, a light supper, or an appetizer. Brie and pears are divine in any setting, and when warm and melty on a crisp crust, they are heavenly.

1 (6-inch) pizza round (prebaked, such as Boboli)
2 teaspoons butter, melted and browned
  Salt and white pepper
3 ounces Brie cheese, cut into $\frac{1}{4}$-inch-thick slices

1 ripe Anjou pear, cored and sliced
2 tablespoons toasted walnut pieces or slivered almonds
  Fresh thyme leaves, or dried thyme

Prep/Baking Time: 15 minutes

Serves 4

1 Preheat the oven to 350°F.

2 Lightly brush the pizza round with some of the browned butter. Sprinkle with salt and pepper to taste.

3 Place the Brie and pear slices decoratively on the pizza round. Brush the pear slices with the remaining browned butter.

4 Tuck the walnut pieces between the cheese and pears. Lightly sprinkle the thyme over all. Place the pizza on a sheet pan and bake for 10 to 15 minutes, until the cheese just begins to melt. Serve hot.

tapas olives

THIS *DIVINO* GLOSSY COMBINATION OF OLIVES, almonds, and orange is presented as part of Spain's famous *tapas* platters. I serve them as part of a "grazing" menu in several small ceramic or wooden bowls. They make welcome hostess gifts when packed in attractive glass jars and will keep for weeks in the refrigerator, but they should be brought to room temperature before serving.

2 (10-ounce) jars pitted large
  green olives, rinsed, drained,
  and patted dry
1/2 cup blanched almonds, lightly
  toasted

5 large garlic cloves, thinly sliced
1 teaspoon red pepper flakes
1 3/4 cups extra-virgin olive oil
  Zest of 1 orange (about
  1 tablespoon)

1 Stuff the olives with the almonds and place in a glass bowl. Combine the remaining ingredients and pour over the olives. Toss gently to coat.

2 Cover and let marinate in the refrigerator for at least 3 days; longer is better. Allow the olives to stand at room temperature for 30 minutes before serving.

3 Transfer the olives to small serving bowls and serve with toothpicks.

Preparation Time:
30 minutes

Marinating Time:
3–6 days

Makes about

3

cups

antipasto with basil vinaigrette

ANTIPASTO IS THE ITALIAN EQUIVALENT OF HORS D'ŒUVRE, meaning "before the meal." Actually, an antipasto platter can serve as an entire meal, and we frequently plan nothing more. The key to success lies in the quality of the ingredients you assemble. An antipasto is sensational for all ages and tastes and for staggered arrival and departure times.

Preparation Time:
30 minutes

Marinating Time:
Overnight

Serves
8-10

1 cup Basil Vinaigrette
(page 75)
1 pound medium mushrooms,
stems trimmed
1 (14-ounce) can artichoke hearts,
drained
1 (16-ounce) can hearts of palm,
cut into 1-inch pieces
12 ounces cherry or grape tomatoes

8 ounces salami, cut into $^1/_2$-inch
cubes
1 pound Italian Fontina cheese
(or other hard cheese), cut into
$^1/_2$-inch cubes
1 pound black olives of your choice
2 loaves sourdough French bread
or Italian semolina bread

1 Pour the vinaigrette into a small bowl and stir in the mushrooms and artichoke hearts. Refrigerate and let marinate overnight.

2 At least 1 hour before serving, combine the hearts of palm, cherry tomatoes, salami, cheese, and olives with the vinaigrette mixture in a large bowl and toss.

3 To serve, allow guests to ladle portions into individual bowls; accompany with chunks of fresh crusty bread.

pinwheels

THESE DELIGHTFUL LITTLE PUFFS can have a variety of fillings. I've presented three possible combinations here: salami with goat cheese, prosciutto with Parmesan, and ham with cream cheese. They are fairly simple to make and can easily be prepped in advance, covered with plastic wrap and refrigerated, and baked just before serving. These may also be baked ahead and warmed in a 200°F oven before serving.

1 (8-ounce) sheet frozen puff
    pastry, thawed
2 ounces chèvre cheese, softened
8 slices hard salami

2 slices prosciutto
3 tablespoons freshly grated
    Parmesan cheese

1 Preheat the oven to 400°F.

2 Unfold the pastry and roll into an 11- by 11-inch square. Cut in half.

3 For the salami pinwheels, spread the chèvre on one of the rolled-out pastry rectangles. Lay the salami on top and roll very tightly, starting on the longest side. Using a very sharp knife, slice into $1/2$-inch rounds. Arrange them on a nonstick baking sheet. For the prosciutto pinwheels, lay the prosciutto slices on top of one of the rectangles. Sprinkle with the Parmesan and roll up as directed.

4 Bake for 10 to 15 minutes until puffed and golden. Cool on a wire rack and serve warm.

Preparation Time:
15 minutes

Baking Time:
10–15 minutes

Makes

36
pinwheels

✕ VARIATION

In one of the puff pastry logs, substitute 2 slices Danish ham for the prosciutto and 1 ounce softened cream cheese for the Parmesan.

wild mushroom
puffs or tarts

THE EARTHY FLAVOR OF WILD MUSHROOMS, smoothed by creamy chèvre and nestled in buttery pastry cups, makes for a divine mouthful. For a great presentation, top each puff with a pea-size dollop of sour cream and a wisp of minced parsley. Frozen puff pastry is a great boon to appetizer and dessert makers. The hard part is done for you; what's left is cutting and baking. Cut bigger rounds to make 12 tarts in regular muffin pans or individual tart pans.

Preparation Time:
30 minutes

Baking Time:
20–25 minutes

Makes

36
small puffs
or

12
little tarts

1 ounce dried porcini mushrooms
  or other earthy dried
  mushrooms
1 (8-ounce) sheet frozen puff
  pastry, thawed
1 tablespoon butter
4 ounces white mushrooms,
  cleaned and chopped
  (about 1 1/4 cups)

2 tablespoons minced shallots
2 tablespoons Sauternes
2 tablespoons chèvre cheese
1/4 teaspoon salt
2 tablespoons chopped
  fresh parsley

1 Place the porcini mushrooms in a small bowl and cover with hot water. Let sit for 20 minutes.

2 Preheat the oven to 400°F.

3 Roll the puff pastry into a 10- by 12-inch rectangle. With a 2-inch fluted biscuit cutter, cut small rounds of dough and poke the dough into mini muffin tins. Scrunch up the scraps and roll again. Cut out more rounds

until you have 36 small fluted cups tucked into the mini muffin tins. (If making small tarts, use a 3-inch biscuit cutter to cut out 12 rounds of pastry.)

4 Drain and chop the porcini mushrooms, reserving the liquid.

5 Melt the butter in a medium skillet over medium heat. Add all the mushrooms and the shallots and sauté for 3 to 5 minutes, stirring occasionally, until the mushrooms give up their moisture and brown slightly.

6 Add the Sauternes and 2 tablespoons of the reserved mushroom liquid. Cook for 1 minute, until the liquid evaporates. Remove from the heat, stir in the chèvre, and sprinkle with the salt. Stir until the chèvre melts, and then add the parsley.

7 Fill each mini cup with $\frac{1}{2}$ teaspoon of the filling. Bake for 15 to 20 minutes, or until the pastry puffs and turns golden. Serve hot or warm. (If making 12 tarts, fill with $1\frac{1}{2}$ teaspoons filling and bake for 20 to 25 minutes.)

MORE PUFFS

You could also fill these puffs with crab, egg salad, or whatever your imagination dictates. And, if you wish to dispense with the puff pastry altogether, cut the crust from large slices of soft whole wheat bread. Cut each piece in quarters, brush with olive oil, and poke into the mini muffin pans. Bake at 400°F for 5 minutes, or until toasted. Spoon the hot mushroom filling inside and serve immediately.

SALADS

SALADS ARE
BEAUTIFUL
AND COLORFUL
AND HELP
MAKE A
NUTRITIOUS
RAINBOW
ON OUR
PLATES.

They are a wonderful accompaniment to most meals, and some can be the main attraction. Fresh salads add crunch and sass to a meal, not to mention all those sought-after vitamins and minerals. While iceberg lettuce with Russian or blue cheese dressing is making its comeback, the choices of greens, vegetables, fruits, and berries for salad, not to mention dressings, are still leaving that pale, watery wedge in the dust.

Even though salad greens are available throughout the year in many forms, it is in spring and on into summer when fresh greens appear in the most profusion, and the choices abound. The realization in spring that the days are growing longer brings the certainty that warm weather and lighter meals are ahead. Spring is a time to walk in a gentle rain, clean out the garden, work in the yard, and just sit outside in the sunshine. It is time to put away the stockpots, take out the grill, go on a picnic, eat fresh asparagus, enjoy lighter meals, and eat salads.

colorful coleslaw

THE COLESLAW DRESSING FROM MY GIRL SCOUT cooking-badge days is as good as the best I have ever eaten. Back then it was magical to add vinegar to evaporated milk and watch it thicken. The trick is to pour it on at the last minute and to be sure the vegetables are crisp and dry.

½ small head red cabbage, finely shredded (about 3 cups)

3 large carrots, peeled and grated

2 tablespoons minced fresh dill

DRESSING

1 cup evaporated milk

2 tablespoons cider vinegar

2 tablespoons sugar

¼ teaspoon salt

¼ cup nonfat plain yogurt (optional)

Preparation Time:
15 minutes

Serves

1 Combine the cabbage, carrots, and dill in a large serving bowl and toss to mix.

2 To make the dressing, combine the milk and vinegar in a small bowl and let it stand for a few minutes, until the milk sours and thickens slightly. Add the sugar, salt, and yogurt, if desired; stir gently until just combined.

3 Pour the dressing over the coleslaw and toss.

SLICING CABBAGE

If your knife skills are great, use a good chef's knife on the cabbage. Otherwise, try the slicing blade on the food processor. For a finer coleslaw, use the processor's shredding disk. I don't recommend the steel blade; you may end up with cabbage mush.

coleslaw with
blue cheese dressing

A CREAMY BLUE CHEESE DRESSING on a cabbage slaw is a nice change from either blue cheese on green salad or traditional coleslaw dressing on cabbage. I love adding coleslaw to meat sandwiches. Try this on a roast beef sandwich or alongside your best burger. It is also nice with salmon.

1/2 small head red cabbage,
    thinly sliced (about 3 cups)
1/4 or 1/2 head green cabbage,
    thinly sliced (about 3 cups)

3 thin carrots, peeled and
    thinly sliced
3/4 cup chopped scallions (2 bunches;
    white and green parts)

DRESSING

3 ounces blue cheese
1/4 cup heavy cream
1/2 cup nonfat plain yogurt
3 tablespoons cider vinegar

3 tablespoons canola oil
2 tablespoons sour cream
1 teaspoon sugar

Preparation Time:
20 minutes

Serves

1 Toss the red and green cabbage together in a large serving bowl. Add the carrots and scallions.

2 To make the dressing, pulse blue cheese and heavy cream together in a food processor until creamy, about 6 pulses. Add the yogurt, vinegar, oil, sour cream, and sugar, and pulse once or twice until mixed.

3 Pour the dressing over the coleslaw and mix thoroughly. Chill until ready to serve.

barley salad

BARLEY IS AN OFTEN FORGOTTEN GRAIN IN THE WEST, where much of it is fed to animals or made into malt. This ancient grain is a dietary staple in many parts of the world, where it is used in soups, porridges, breads, and drinks. Its sweet, nutty, slightly earthy flavor makes it a tasty grain for salads and side dishes. At the supermarket, you are most likely to find pearled barley, which has had the husk removed and is suitable for this recipe.

2 1/2 cups chicken stock
1 1/4 cups barley
2 tablespoons chopped
    sun-dried tomatoes
2 large ripe tomatoes (optional),
    chopped and seeded
3 scallions, minced
    (white and green parts)
1/2 cup minced fresh parsley

3/4 cup mixed chopped red, yellow,
    and green bell peppers
1/4 cup extra-virgin olive oil
1/3 cup red wine vinegar
    Salt and freshly ground
    black pepper
2 tablespoons crumbled
    feta cheese

Preparation Time:
20 minutes

Cooking Time:
30 minutes

Serves
8

1 Bring the chicken stock to a boil in a large saucepan. Add the barley, cover, and cook over low heat for 30 minutes, until the grain has puffed and absorbed the liquid.

2 Fluff with a fork and cool slightly. Add the remaining ingredients and toss well to mix. Serve the salad at room temperature in an attractive bowl.

cucumber raita

A COOL, REFRESHING ANTIDOTE to spicy dishes, raita can calm the heat of curries and tandooris with its soothing blend of yogurt and cucumber. Serve it as a salad or side dish with chicken, fish, or meat.

4 cucumbers, peeled and grated
1 teaspoon ground cumin
1 tablespoon cider vinegar

1 teaspoon prepared horseradish
1–1½ cups nonfat plain yogurt

1 Put the grated cucumber in a medium bowl and refrigerate for about 30 minutes.

2 Drain off any water that collects in the bowl. Add the cumin, vinegar, horseradish, and yogurt. Stir well and serve cold.

Preparation Time:
10 minutes

Chilling Time:
30 minutes

Serves

8

MENU FOR AN INDIAN MEAL AT HOME

- Tandoori Chicken (page 147)
- Red Lentils (page 170)
- Basmati Rice
- Cucumber Raita

- Mango chutney
- Orange Sherbet with Orange Slices (page 227)

chilled **couscous** with radishes and **pine nuts**

COUSCOUS, A CULINARY STAPLE IN MUCH OF NORTH AFRICA, tastes like the happy product of a marriage between pasta and rice. Its light and mild flavor blends perfectly with the orange juice and the zip of the radishes to produce a very attractive and appealing side dish. Shop for a brand that is made from pure semolina flour, as couscous made with regular flour may become mushy.

$^3/_4$ cup chicken stock
$^1/_2$ cup water
$^1/_2$ cup uncooked couscous
$^3/_4$ cup orange juice
1 tablespoon orange zest
$^1/_2$ cup chopped fresh parsley

3 tablespoons extra-virgin olive oil
3 tablespoons cider vinegar
1$^1/_2$ cups thinly sliced radishes
$^1/_3$ cup pine nuts, toasted
Salt and freshly ground
black pepper

Prep/Cooking Time:
15 minutes

Serves

1 Bring the chicken stock and water to a boil in a medium saucepan. Add the couscous slowly, stirring constantly, until all the liquid has been absorbed. Remove from the heat and let stand for 2 minutes.

2 Turn the couscous onto a large baking sheet; spread it evenly and let cool to room temperature. When cool, separate any clumps and transfer to a large mixing bowl. Add $^1/_2$ cup of the orange juice, the orange zest, and the parsley, and toss. (The couscous can be refrigerated at this point for a day or two if you like.)

3 Before serving, whisk together the remaining $^1/_4$ cup orange juice, the oil, and the vinegar, and toss with the couscous mixture. Add radishes and pine nuts and toss again. Season to taste with salt and pepper and serve.

green and orange salad

THE WATERCRESS GIVES THIS REFRESHING SALAD a tartness that makes it a perfect partner for the Chicken with Wild Rice and Cherries on page 123. It also works well with egg dishes on a brunch menu.

2 cups fresh orange sections
1 red onion, thinly sliced and
    separated into rings
1/4 cup red wine vinegar
1/4 cup extra-virgin olive oil
2 tablespoons finely chopped
    fresh parsley

2 bunches watercress, washed,
    dried, and tough stems
    removed
6 cups coarsely torn mixed salad
    lettuce (Bibb, romaine, or leaf),
    washed and dried

1 Combine the orange sections with the onion rings in a medium bowl. Whisk together the vinegar and oil and pour over the orange-onion mixture. Sprinkle with parsley and refrigerate for 2 hours, tossing occasionally.

2 When ready to serve, toss the watercress with the lettuce in a large, shallow bowl. Spread the greens evenly over the bottom of the bowl and arrange the oranges and onions on top. Drizzle the dressing over all and serve immediately.

Preparation Time:
30 minutes

Chilling Time:
2 hours

Serves

spinach and arugula salad with strawberries and orange dressing

ARUGULA IS A WONDERFULLY SPICY-TASTING GREEN with an incredible, pungent aroma. It is sometimes expensive to buy in the market but (fortunately for gardeners) very easy to grow in the garden. Fresh strawberries brighten the color and flavor of spinach and other greens. While they are often available in the market, they are best in the summertime, when in season. If there are no nut allergies, toss a few toasted pecans into the salad bowl. To make a heartier salad, add canned cannellini beans, rinsed and drained.

1 pound fresh spinach, washed,
   dried, and stems trimmed
1 bunch arugula, washed and dried
1 small red onion, thinly sliced
3 tablespoons canola oil

2 tablespoons orange juice
  Salt and freshly ground
   black pepper
1 pint fresh strawberries, washed,
   hulled, and cut in half

Preparation Time:
15 minutes

Serves

1 Tear the spinach and arugula into bite-size pieces; place in a large, shallow salad bowl. Add the onion and toss lightly.

2 Whisk together the oil and orange juice; season with salt and pepper. Pour the dressing over the salad and toss well. Scatter the strawberries artfully over the top of the salad and serve with a flourish.

spinach cucumber salad with lime dressing

HERE IS AN UNCOMPLICATED, BRIGHT, AND REFRESHING SALAD to clear the palate after a hearty meal. Try it alongside a creamy soup for a satisfying lunch or supper.

$^1/_2$–$^3/_4$ pound fresh spinach, washed, dried, and stems trimmed
2 cucumbers, peeled and chopped
1 small red onion, thinly sliced

DRESSING

$^1/_2$ cup nonfat plain yogurt
Juice of 2 limes (about 3 tablespoons)
1 tablespoon olive oil

$^1/_4$ teaspoon ground cumin
Salt and freshly ground black pepper

Preparation Time: 15 minutes

Serves

Arrange the spinach on a platter; top with the cucumbers and onions. Whisk together the dressing ingredients and drizzle over the salad. Serve immediately.

fresh **tomatoes** with **herbed** caper **vinaigrette**

FRESH TOMATOES FROM THE GARDEN hardly need perking up, but when they are in season, gild them with this fresh herbaceous dressing for a summer treat.

$1/3$ cup white wine vinegar
1 tablespoon lemon juice
1 teaspoon Dijon mustard
Salt and freshly ground
    black pepper
$2/3$ cup extra-virgin olive oil

2 tablespoons chopped
    fresh parsley
1 tablespoon chopped scallion
1 teaspoon capers
1 garlic clove, minced
4–6 large ripe tomatoes

Preparation Time:
10 minutes

Serves

4–6

1 Whisk together the vinegar, lemon juice, and mustard. Season with salt and pepper to taste. Gradually blend in the olive oil. Whisk in the parsley, scallion, capers, and garlic. Alternatively, put all of the ingredients except the capers in a food processor or blender and blend at high speed. Stir in the capers. Store the dressing in the refrigerator for up to 3 days.

2 When ready to serve, cut the tomatoes into slices or wedges, arrange them on a platter, and drizzle the dressing over the top.

crunchy **waldorf** salad

WHAT SAYS "FALL" BETTER THAN WALDORF SALAD? Crisp apples, crunchy celery, and sweet, succulent grapes folded into a tangy blue cheese dressing and topped with toasted nuts give you the ultimate fall salad. Use red and green apples and red and green grapes to make a colorful palette on your plate. It is just possible that salad-averse children will leap to the table to eat this luscious mix.

2 tart red apples, cored and
    chopped into $^1/_2$-inch chunks
2 Granny Smith apples, cored and
    chopped into $^1/_2$-inch chunks
3 celery stalks, diced

$^1/_2$ cup seedless red grapes,
    cut in half
$^1/_2$ cup seedless green grapes,
    cut in half
$^1/_3$ cup chopped walnuts, toasted

DRESSING
$^1/_2$ cup nonfat plain yogurt
$^1/_4$ cup light mayonnaise
$^1/_4$ cup crumbled blue cheese
2 tablespoons lemon juice

Preparation Time:
15 minutes

Serves

1 Toss the apples, celery, grapes, and walnuts together in a large serving bowl.

2 Stir the dressing ingredients together in a small bowl until smooth. Pour over the salad and mix well. Chill in the refrigerator until ready to serve.

greek shrimp salad

LOTS OF FEATHERY DILL, FRESH LEMON JUICE, and healthy, crisp watercress are a perfect match for the chilled shrimp and tangy feta. Serve the salad with a warm loaf of sourdough bread for a sensational yet simple lunch or supper. This utterly delicious main-course salad has the fresh taste of summer all year round. Ahead of time, clean and store the watercress in the refrigerator with its stems in water and the leaves loosely covered with a plastic bag. The rest of the salad can be prepared early in the day and refrigerated; just hold off on adding the watercress until you are ready to serve.

1 large red onion, quartered and
   thinly sliced
2 pounds cooked shrimp, shelled,
   deveined, and chilled
1 cup crumbled feta cheese
   (about 4 ounces)

2 bunches watercress, washed,
   dried, and stems trimmed
1 pint cherry or grape tomatoes

Preparation Time:
30 minutes

Serves
6

DRESSING

$\frac{1}{3}$ cup finely chopped fresh dill
$\frac{1}{4}$ cup lemon juice
$\frac{1}{4}$ cup olive oil
 1 garlic clove, minced

Dash of Tabasco sauce
Salt and freshly ground
   black pepper

1 Spread the onion slices in the bottom of a large salad bowl. Scatter the shrimp over the onions. Sprinkle with the feta and watercress. Scatter the tomatoes over the salad.

2 Combine the dressing ingredients in a bottle and shake well.

3 Pour the dressing over the salad and toss to combine.

endive and radish salad with raspberry vinaigrette

HERE IS A QUICK, CRUNCHY SALAD WITH SUBTLE LAYERS OF FLAVOR that can be put together at the last minute. Belgian endive's creamy color belies its slightly bitter taste. Arugula adds its peppery notes to the sharpness of the radishes. All these come together in a wonderful blend that is brightened by the color and sweetness of oranges to make a spectacular stand-alone salad.

1 small head romaine lettuce, washed and dried

1 small bunch arugula, washed and dried

2 bunches radishes, trimmed and chopped

2 Belgian endives, thinly sliced

1 small red onion, thinly sliced

3 oranges, peeled, pith removed, and cut into sections

2 tablespoons walnut oil

1/4 cup raspberry vinegar

2 tablespoons crumbled feta cheese

Freshly ground white pepper

1 Prepare individual servings by evenly dividing the romaine and arugula among 8 salad plates.

2 Toss the radishes, endive, onion, and oranges together in a large bowl. Drizzle with the oil and toss. Sprinkle with the vinegar and toss again.

3 Spoon the mixture onto the plates, sprinkle with the feta, season with pepper, and serve immediately.

Preparation Time: 15 minutes

Serves

curried red lentil salad

THIS IS AN ALL-TIME FAVORITE SALAD WITH A SPICY KICK. Curry is a blend of many spices, which in India are purchased separately in the market and ground together. Curry powder is an attempt to replicate the blend of flavors with a combination of ground spices. If your spice rack cannot produce the variety needed for this recipe, you can substitute curry powder for some or all of the spices. Check the curry powder label first, however, to see what you are substituting. If you do mix the suggested spices, you will be rewarded by a rich blend that complements the mild taste of the lentils.

2 cups water
1 pound red lentils, rinsed and
    picked over
1 cup currants

$\frac{1}{3}$ cup capers
1 medium red onion, thinly sliced
    Fresh lettuce leaves, washed
    and dried, for serving

Preparation Time:
30 minutes

Setting Time:
Several hours
to overnight

Serves

VINAIGRETTE
$\frac{1}{2}$ cup tarragon wine vinegar
1 tablespoon sugar
$\frac{1}{2}$ teaspoon salt
1 teaspoon ground cumin
1 teaspoon dry mustard
$\frac{1}{2}$ teaspoon ground cardamom
$\frac{1}{2}$ teaspoon ground coriander
$\frac{1}{2}$ teaspoon ground mace

$\frac{1}{2}$ teaspoon ground turmeric
$\frac{1}{4}$ teaspoon cayenne pepper
$\frac{1}{4}$ teaspoon ground cinnamon
$\frac{1}{4}$ teaspoon ground cloves
$\frac{1}{4}$ teaspoon ground nutmeg
    About 2 teaspoons freshly
    ground black pepper
$\frac{3}{4}$ cup canola oil

1 Bring the water to a boil, add the lentils, and cook until they are just tender, about 10 minutes. You don't want them to be mushy. Rinse and drain the cooked lentils.

2 While the lentils cook, make the vinaigrette. Combine all the vinaigrette ingredients except the oil in a small bowl; mix well. Slowly whisk in the oil, not for a thick emulsion but to combine well.

3 Combine the lentils and vinaigrette in a large bowl and allow to sit for several hours or overnight in the refrigerator.

4 Several hours before serving, add the currants, capers, and onions to the lentils and let marinate. Serve the salad on fresh lettuce leaves arranged on a large plate, chilled or at room temperature.

NOTE: Currants are actually dried Zante grapes. Do not use fresh currants.

MENU FOR A MEMORIAL DAY PICNIC

- Healthy Nachos (page 42) with Kate's Fresh Salsa (page 33)
- Grilled Lamb Pocket Burgers with Chopped Cucumber Salad (page 96)
- Curried Red Lentil Salad
- Vanilla Frozen Yogurt with Fresh Strawberries and Hot Bittersweet Chocolate Sauce (page 236)

italian bean salad

CANNELLINI BEANS ARE ONE OF MY FAVORITE INGREDIENTS in soups and salads. The small package of fiber and nutrition softens the bite of spinach or arugula and adds a mild flavor and creamy texture to sharp, crisp salads. The dressing is lower in fat than many salad dressings. The thickened chicken broth does not replicate the flavor of fine olive oil, but it gives a nice creamy quality to the dressing.

Preparation Time:
20 minutes

Chilling Time:
Several hours

Serves

2 (16-ounce) cans cannellini beans, rinsed and drained
1 medium red onion, thinly sliced
3 canned artichoke hearts, drained and quartered
1/3 cup black olives, sliced
1 teaspoon dried oregano
1 cup shredded arugula (optional), washed and dried

1/2 teaspoon cornstarch
1/4 cup chicken broth
4 tablespoons red wine vinegar
2 tablespoons extra-virgin olive oil
Salt and freshly ground black pepper

1 Mix together the beans, onion, artichoke hearts, olives, oregano, and arugula in a medium bowl.

2 Combine the cornstarch and chicken broth in a small saucepan; cook over low heat until the mixture thickens, then cook for a few minutes more. Cool slightly, and then whisk in the vinegar and oil. Pour over the bean mixture and toss lightly. Season to taste with salt and pepper and serve at room temperature.

✕ VARIATION

Add quartered Roma tomatoes and capers instead of olives. For a heartier salad, add a 4-ounce can of tuna packed in olive oil.

black bean and fresh tomato salad

THIS IS ANOTHER WONDERFUL SUMMERTIME TOMATO SALAD. It could make a vegetarian main course (without the chicken broth, of course) or a great addition to grilled chicken, fish, or meat. The beans can be cooked ahead of time. Alternatively, you could use a can of black beans, rinsed and drained; if you do that, mince the garlic and cilantro and add them to the bean mix so that you don't miss out on the flavors of the bean cooking broth.

1 cup dried black beans
3 cups chicken stock
1 garlic clove, crushed
1/2 teaspoon ground cumin
3 fresh cilantro sprigs
2 tablespoons good-quality olive oil, plus more for serving
1/2 cup minced fresh parsley

Salt and freshly ground black pepper
8 red lettuce leaves (or other large-leaf lettuce)
3 large ripe tomatoes, sliced
Balsamic vinegar
Handful of basil leaves, shredded

1 Put the beans, chicken stock, garlic, cumin, and cilantro in a large saucepan and bring to a boil. Lower the heat and simmer, partially covered, for 1 1/2 to 2 hours, or until the beans are tender. Add water if necessary to keep the beans from becoming dry.

2 Rinse and drain the beans and toss with the 2 tablespoons olive oil and the parsley. Season with salt and pepper.

3 Place the lettuce leaves attractively on a platter. Arrange the tomatoes on top, drizzle with the vinegar and more olive oil, and sprinkle with the basil. Scatter the beans over all. Serve at room temperature.

Preparation Time:
15 minutes

Cooking Time:
2 hours

Serves

beet, orange, and fennel salad with gorgonzola and a savory vinaigrette

THE COLORS OF THIS SALAD ARE FABULOUS and the deep flavor magnificent; a far cry from the canned or boiled-to-death beets of old. If golden beets are available, use those and blood oranges to get the best color contrast. This sensational salad is well worth the effort and deserves to be served as a separate course for your favorite friends. Prepare the ingredients ahead of time and combine at the last minute.

Preparation Time:
20 minutes

Cooking Time:
45 minutes

Serves
4

1 pound beets
1 teaspoon salt
½ fennel bulb
2 navel oranges

1 head butter lettuce, washed and dried
⅓ cup crumbled Gorgonzola cheese (2 ounces)

JANE'S VINAIGRETTE

1 tablespoon balsamic vinegar
2 tablespoons cider vinegar
2 tablespoons maple syrup
1 tablespoon minced shallots

1 garlic clove, minced
1 teaspoon Dijon mustard
¾ cup olive oil

1 Wash and trim the beets, leaving about 1 inch of root. Fill a large pot with about 2 inches of water and bring to a boil. Add the salt and beets. Return to a boil, reduce the heat, and simmer for about 45 minutes, or until the beets are easily pierced with a fork. Drain, and, when cool enough to handle, slip the skins off the beets and cut into ½-inch pieces. Set aside.

2 Trim the fennel and slice it very thinly. Use a 1-mm slicing blade on the food processor or careful knife work to get these thin slices. Set aside.

3 Peel and section the oranges and set aside.

4 To make the vinaigrette, combine the vinegars, syrup, shallots, garlic, and mustard in a food processor or blender. With the motor running, pour in the oil in a thin stream. Pour the dressing into a jar and refrigerate until ready to use.

5 To compose the salad, combine the beets, fennel, and oranges in a medium bowl and gently toss. Drizzle about 1/4 cup of the vinaigrette over the vegetables. Use more dressing if you wish, or save the remainder for other salads.

6 Arrange one or two of the lettuce leaves on each of four plates. Divide the salad among the plates. Scatter the Gorgonzola on each salad and serve.

ABOUT BEETS ✕

In supermarkets and farmers' markets, it is sometimes possible to buy beets of different varieties and colors. There are traditional deep red beets, golden beets, and Chioggia beets, which are Italian heirloom beets that are white and red. It makes for a lovely presentation to have a variety of colors, so if they are available, I urge you to use two or three colors of beets.

You may also roast beets, which adds another layer of flavor to the salad.

Wash and trim them, rub with oil, and place them in a roasting pan with about 1/2 cup of water.

Cover with aluminum foil and roast at 425°F for about 1 hour, or until easily pierced with a fork.

Let cool, peel, and proceed with the recipe.

broccoli **cashew** salad

THIS DELIGHTFUL CRUNCHY SALAD ADDS COLOR and texture to any meal. My daughter Wendy serves it regularly to the stream of teens and preteens who swarm through her house. Wendy reports, "Everyone likes it, it is easy, it is healthy, and you can serve it all year round." This one is definitely a keeper. Add the dressing at the last minute to keep the broccoli bright and green.

1 head broccoli, trimmed and cut
   into bite-size pieces
1 red bell pepper
1 green bell pepper

2 carrots
⅓ cup dressing (see below)
1 cup cashew pieces,
   lightly toasted

Preparation Time:
25 minutes

Chilling Time:
1 hour

Serves

DRESSING

½ cup olive oil
¼ cup red wine vinegar
2 teaspoons soy sauce

1 garlic clove, minced
1 teaspoon Dijon mustard
   Freshly ground black pepper

1 Bring a large pot of salted water to a boil. Using a steamer basket, steam the broccoli for about 5 minutes, or just until tender. Drain, plunge into ice water to cool, and drain again. Add to a large bowl.

2 Core and seed the red and green peppers and cut into ½-inch cubes. Peel and coarsely shred the carrots. Add to the bowl with the broccoli.

3 Combine the dressing ingredients in a small bowl and whisk until well blended. Pour ⅓ cup of the dressing over the vegetables. Toss, add more dressing if desired, and refrigerate for 1 hour.

4 When ready to serve, add the cashews and toss again.

pear, pecan, and blue cheese salad

THIS IS ONE OF MY FAVORITE SIMPLE SALADS. It has some sweet, some tang, and a bit of crunch and is a cut above a plain old tossed salad. I've given instructions for serving it either mixed in a salad bowl or arranged on plates as a composed salad. The vinaigrette for the beet salad (page 68) is perfect with this one, too. Make extra toasted pecans and store them in an airtight container for later use.

1 small head Boston lettuce, washed and dried

1 small head red lettuce or the equivalent amount of mixed baby greens or mâche, washed and dried

3 ripe Anjou pears

⅓ cup pecans, chopped and toasted

3 ounces blue cheese or Roquefort cheese

⅓ cup Jane's Vinaigrette (page 68)

1 For a composed salad, artfully arrange the lettuce leaves on six salad plates. Slice the pears into 8 slices each and fan out 4 slices over each plate. Scatter the pecans on top. Cut the cheese into 4 slices and place 1 on each plate. Drizzle each plate with the vinaigrette and serve.

2 To make a tossed salad, tear the heads of lettuce into a large salad bowl. Cut the pears into chunks and add to the bowl. Add the nuts and crumble the cheese into the bowl. Sprinkle with the vinaigrette, toss, and serve.

Preparation Time:
15 minutes

Serves
6

caesar salad for all

CAESAR SALAD HAS A HUGE FAN CLUB. My daughter Liza does a lot of casual family entertaining, and her "Caesar bar" works beautifully. Kids, teens, parents, and grandparents alike can find some part of the lineup they enjoy. Add a loaf of warm crusty garlic bread for total satisfaction. By the way, the salad is not named after Julius but after its creator, Caesar Cardini, an Italian restaurateur in Tijuana, Mexico, who created the salad in 1924.

Preparation Time:
15 minutes

Serves

4

(increase in
multiples to feed
a crowd)

1 pound cooked boneless, skinless chicken breasts

1 (10-ounce) package hearts of romaine lettuce pieces, washed and dried

$\frac{1}{4}$ cup Caesar Dressing (see next page for recipe)

2 cups Homemade Croutons (see next page for recipe)

$\frac{1}{4}$ cup freshly grated Parmesan cheese

Anchovy fillets (optional)

1   Slice the chicken breasts $\frac{1}{4}$ inch thick and arrange on a plate. Toss the lettuce with the dressing in a medium salad bowl. Put the croutons and the grated cheese in small serving bowls. Place the anchovies on a small plate, if desired.

2   Arrange the plates and bowls in a row, starting with the lettuce, and invite guests to serve themselves.

homemade **croutons**

ANYTHING GOES, FROM WHITE TO WHOLE GRAIN, as long as you use a good-quality bread. This is a great way to enjoy leftover baguettes.

4–5 tablespoons olive oil
  2 garlic cloves, minced
  2 cups 1-inch cubes of bread

1 Heat the oil in a large nonstick skillet over medium-high heat. Add the garlic and bread cubes and sauté until lightly browned on all sides, tossing them well (6 to 8 minutes). Do not let the bread or garlic burn. Remove to paper towels to drain and cool.

2 Store the croutons in an airtight plastic bag at room temperature for up to 1 week. For longer storage, freeze for up to 6 months.

Preparation/
Cooking Time:
10 minutes

Makes

cups

CAESAR DRESSING

Preparation Time: 10 minutes • Makes ¹/₂ cup

This tangy, light dressing avoids the traditional eggs and anchovy paste. Its fresh sizzle comes from the combination of mustards plus a hint of tarragon.

- 4 tablespoons tarragon vinegar
- 4 tablespoons olive oil
- 2 teaspoons Dijon mustard
- 2 garlic cloves, minced
- 2 teaspoons sugar
- 1 teaspoon salt

- 1 teaspoon freshly ground black pepper
- ¹/₂ teaspoon dry mustard

Combine all the ingredients in a bottle and shake well.

BIG GREEN SALAD

We love to create Big Green Salads featuring seasonal vegetables and fruits. Here are some flavorful, fresh-from-the-garden combinations. Experiment with our favorite dressings or simply toss your salad with some good olive oil, then add vinegar or lemon juice and toss again. Finally, grind some black pepper over the creation and serve.

SPRING AND SUMMER SALAD:

- Tender greens and/or lettuces
- Arugula
- Scallions
- Strawberries and other seasonal berries
- Avocado
- Fresh peas
- Sugar snap peas or snow peas

SUMMER AND FALL SALAD:

- Crispy, crunchy lettuce, like romaine hearts and heads of red and green
- Garden-ripe tomatoes
- Cucumbers
- Sweet onions
- Carrots
- Red bell peppers
- Green beans

FALL AND WINTER SALAD:

- Sturdy heads of lettuce, bitter greens such as frisée and curly endive
- Pears and apples
- Nuts
- Celery
- Root vegetables, such as beets and carrots

4 great dressings

✕ POPPY SEED DRESSING

1 cup canola oil
$\frac{1}{2}$ cup cranberry juice
$\frac{1}{4}$ cup honey
1 tablespoon dry mustard

1 tablespoon grated onion
1 teaspoon salt
$1\frac{1}{2}$ tablespoons poppy seeds

Combine the oil, juice, honey, dry mustard, onion, and salt in a glass jar; shake until the honey is well blended with other ingredients. Add the poppy seeds and shake well.

✕ BASIL VINAIGRETTE

½ cup red wine vinegar

1 teaspoon Dijon mustard

1 garlic clove, minced

1½ cups extra-virgin olive oil

1 tablespoon chopped fresh basil,
  or 1 teaspoon dried

1 tablespoon chopped fresh
  oregano, or 1 teaspoon dried

Salt and freshly ground
  black pepper

Whisk the vinegar, mustard, and garlic together in a small bowl. Slowly add the oil, whisking constantly. Stir in the herbs; season to taste with salt and pepper. Store in a tightly sealed jar in the refrigerator for up to 2 days. Serve at room temperature.

✕ CUMIN VINAIGRETTE

5 tablespoons extra-virgin olive oil

1 tablespoon red wine vinegar

1 tablespoon orange juice

1 small garlic clove, minced

4 teaspoons ground cumin

1 teaspoon sugar

Whisk together all the ingredients. Cover and let stand for at least 1 hour, or refrigerate for up to 2 days. Serve this sprightly dressing on a light salad of orange and avocado slices or other citrusy salads.

✕ JEANNE'S SALAD DRESSING

1⅓ cups canola oil

⅔ cup cider vinegar

6 garlic cloves, minced

1 tablespoon Worcestershire sauce

1 tablespoon lemon juice

1 tablespoon sugar

1 teaspoon dry mustard

1 teaspoon salt

1 teaspoon freshly ground
  black pepper

Combine all the ingredients in a medium bowl and mix well. Taste and correct for sweetness and seasoning. Store in a glass jar in the refrigerator for up to 3 days. Allow it to sit at room temperature for 30 minutes before using.

SOUPS

STEAMING BOWLS OF FLAVORFUL SOUP ARE A SIMPLE, WARMING WAY TO ENTERTAIN ON CHILLY EVENINGS.

It's mostly during cold weather that I think of gathering people around comforting soup meals. At the onset of fall, before the growing time ends, there is a glorious display of nature's brilliance in many parts of the country. Few leaves have dropped to the ground, and the bright-colored ones are set against a backdrop of green. Gradually, the vibrant color spreads across the landscape. But fall is just a moment in the year, and then it's gone.

Wonderful, heavy-skinned vegetables appear in markets, to be turned into chunky stews and creamy soups. As days grow shorter, it's time to move inside and create those cozy, tummy-warming meals. While there are many bright, light, summer soups, the ones that follow are the hearty ones, fit for the main event.

Clearly, soup can be the first course of an elegant dinner party, but I think of soup more as a main course. Entertaining around a soup-centered meal is about as easy as it gets, and a wonderful way to entertain friends casually. Soups by their nature are great make-ahead meals. Add a good loaf of bread and a salad and you have a wonderful meal to share with friends.

apple pumpkin soup

ROASTING FRESH PUMPKIN GIVES AN ADDED LAYER OF FLAVOR, and, when puréed, is like velvet. If you don't have the time, substitute 3 cups of canned pumpkin. In either case, you will have a lovely, smooth pumpkin soup. Serve it with bran muffins and a big salad for a simple supper or hearty lunch.

1½ pounds fresh pumpkin, seeds
  and fibers removed and cut into
  big chunks
2 tablespoons olive oil
1 tablespoon butter
1 cup chopped onion
½ large Granny Smith apple, peeled,
  cored, and sliced

2 teaspoons minced,
  fresh gingerroot
1 teaspoon salt
1 cup apple juice or apple cider
3 cups chicken broth
¼ cup nonfat plain yogurt (optional)
⅛ teaspoon white pepper
1 teaspoon lemon juice

Preparation Time:
30 minutes

Cooking Time:
1 hour 10 minutes

Serves

6

1 Preheat the oven to 400°F.

2 Place the pumpkin chunks in a large roasting pan and rub them with 1 tablespoon of the olive oil. Roast for 45 minutes, or until easily pierced with a fork. Cool, remove peel, and mash slightly. You should have about 3 cups.

3 Heat the remaining 1 tablespoon olive oil and the butter in a Dutch oven over medium heat. Add the onions and sauté, stirring, for about 3 minutes, or until the onions begin to soften. Add the apples and ginger and cook for another 5 minutes. Add the pumpkin, sprinkle with salt, and pour the apple juice and broth over all. Bring to a boil, turn down to a simmer, cover, and cook for 20 minutes.

4 Cool the soup slightly and purée in batches in a blender. Return the soup to the pot and taste. Add the yogurt, if desired. Heat gently, and season with the white pepper and lemon juice. Serve hot.

zucchini bisque

THIS DELICATE AND DELICIOUS PALE GREEN SOUP successfully pairs zucchini with basil and a hint of nutmeg. It is no trick to make and will probably become a regular, served either hot or chilled. Choose slender young zucchini. If you decide not to add the cream, you might use a little less nutmeg and basil.

4 tablespoons ($^1/_2$ stick) butter	2 tablespoons dried basil
2 medium onions, chopped	2 teaspoons sea salt
3 pounds zucchini, sliced no thicker than $^1/_2$ inch thick	Freshly ground black pepper to taste
5 cups chicken broth	$^1/_2$ cup heavy cream (optional)
1 teaspoon ground nutmeg	

1   Melt the butter in a large stockpot over medium-high heat. Add the onions and sauté until they soften, 6 to 8 minutes.

2   Stir in the zucchini and chicken broth. Bring the mixture to a boil over high heat. Turn down the heat and let simmer for 30 minutes. Remove from the heat and let sit until cool enough to handle.

3   Working in batches, purée the soup on low in blender or food processor until smooth.

4   Blend in the nutmeg, basil, salt, and pepper to taste. (The soup may be frozen at this point.)

5   To serve, heat the soup and stir in cream, if desired.

Preparation Time:
20 minutes

Cooking Time:
30 minutes

Serves

6-8

tuscan bean and chard soup

THIS SIMPLE SOUP IS SATISFYING TO THE SOUL as well as to the palate. Easy to make and packed with flavor and nutrition, it is a wonderful way to get good greens and legumes into your tummy. Rainbow chard or ruby chard will add a reddish tone to the soup. This is not a problem, but I prefer to use green chard. And, of course, if you have homemade chicken stock, use it. For a vegetarian version, use vegetable stock.

Preparation Time:
15 minutes

Cooking Time:
10 minutes

Serves

1 tablespoon olive oil, plus
   more for drizzling
1 medium onion, chopped
2 garlic cloves, minced
½ teaspoon salt
2 chicken sausages (optional),
   cut into ½-inch slices and
   then half-moons

4 cups chicken broth
1 bunch Swiss chard (about
   1 pound), washed, ribs removed,
   and sliced into ¼-inch ribbons
1 (16-ounce) can cannellini beans,
   rinsed and drained
¼ cup freshly grated Parmesan
   cheese

1 Heat the olive oil in a Dutch oven over medium heat. Add the onion and sauté, stirring, until it starts to soften. Add the garlic and salt and continue cooking until the onions are soft and translucent, about 2 minutes longer. Add the sausage pieces, if using, and cook for 5 minutes, until they begin to brown.

2 Add the broth and scrape any browned bits from the bottom of the pot. Add the chard and bring to a boil. Cover, turn the heat down to a simmer, and cook for about 5 minutes, or until the chard wilts. Add the beans and cook for another 2 minutes, until they are warmed.

3 Serve the hot soup in bowls, sprinkling each serving with a tablespoon of Parmesan and a drizzle of olive oil.

PREPARING SWISS CHARD

Plunge chard leaves into a sink full of cold water; lift out chard, letting grit settle to the bottom. Drain. Fold a chard leaf in half along the rib and lay on a cutting board. With a large knife, cut the thick part of the rib away from the leaves.

Repeat with each leaf. Use the ribs another time, in a stir-fry, or just sauté them in olive oil. Stack the leaves and slice through them to create $1/4$-inch ribbons.

MENU FOR A TASTE OF ITALY DINNER ✕

- Tuscan Bean and Chard Soup
- Tuscan Pork Tenderloin (page 145)
- Green Beans with Pine Nut Oil (page 171)
- Pear Almond Galette (page 238)

cream of **chicken** soup

THIS IS A GREAT SOUP TO MAKE WITH LEFTOVERS from Roasted Rosemary Chicken (page 152). Make chicken stock in the same way as you do turkey stock (page 87), using the bones from a roast chicken instead of a turkey. This soup is a warmly satisfying blend of chicken and vegetables that I like to take to people in need of comfort. Years ago, my friend Judy served a similar soup to me, and it's been on my list ever since. I've found that it's a great way to use up leftover chicken and rice.

1 tablespoon butter
2 tablespoons canola oil
3 cups cooked chicken, shredded
   or cut into large chunks
1 teaspoon salt
$\frac{1}{4}$ teaspoon dried thyme
$\frac{1}{4}$ cup all-purpose flour
4 cups chicken stock, canned
   or homemade

1 cup peeled and sliced carrots,
   precooked until almost tender
$1\frac{1}{2}$ cups cooked rice
1 cup small frozen peas
$\frac{1}{8}$ teaspoon white pepper
$\frac{1}{4}$–$\frac{1}{2}$ cup half-and-half (optional)

Cooking Time:
15 minutes

Serves
6

1 Heat the butter and oil in a Dutch oven over medium heat. Add the chicken and cook for 1 minute, stirring and turning. Stir in the salt and thyme, and then sprinkle with the flour. Cook for 1 minute and then add 3 cups of the stock. Increase the heat slightly and cook, stirring often, until the mixture bubbles and thickens, about 5 minutes.

2 Add the carrots, rice, peas, and pepper, and enough remaining stock to make the consistency you like. Reduce the heat and simmer for 5 minutes. Add the half-and-half, if desired.

lemon soup

THE ORZO (A TINY, RICE-SIZE SEMOLINA PASTA) AND BROTH can be prepared in advance and the eggs added at the last minute for this light, refreshing soup.

5 cups chicken broth
3 cups plus 2 tablespoons water
$1/2$ cup orzo

4 egg whites
2 egg yolks
Juice of 2 lemons

1 Bring the broth and 3 cups water to a boil in a large saucepan. Add the orzo and cook over medium heat for 15 to 20 minutes, until the pasta is tender but not soggy.

2 Beat the egg whites with the remaining 2 tablespoons water in a large bowl until soft peaks form.

3 Beat the egg yolks with the lemon juice in a small bowl; fold into the egg whites.

4 Add some of the hot broth to the egg mixture and stir gently to warm the mixture. Add all of the egg mixture to the hot broth and simmer, stirring constantly, until the soup thickens slightly. Serve at once.

Prep/Cooking Time:
30 minutes

Serves

soupe au **pistou** (french vegetable soup)

HERE IS A SIMPLE VERSION of this wonderful French Mediterranean soup. Pistou, the French version of pesto, turns a plain vegetable soup into a richly flavored, aromatic pleasure. While it is not a thick, heavy soup, you will feel that you have had a wonderful meal after eating a bowl of it accompanied by French bread.

Prep/Cooking Time:
1 hour

Serves

1½ quarts water
1 cup diced carrots
1 cup diced potatoes
1 cup diced onions
½ teaspoon salt
½ cup green beans

1 cup cooked or canned and
    drained navy or kidney beans
⅓ cup broken uncooked spaghetti
1 slice French bread
    Freshly ground black pepper
    Pinch of saffron

PISTOU

2 garlic cloves, mashed
2 tablespoons tomato paste
2 tablespoons finely chopped fresh
    basil, or 1 teaspoon dried

¼ cup freshly grated
    Parmesan cheese
3 tablespoons olive oil

1 Combine the water, carrots, potatoes, and onions in a stockpot; bring to a boil and turn the heat down to medium-low. Simmer for 30 minutes, or until the vegetables are tender. Season with salt. (This step can be done ahead of time.)

2 Add the green beans, navy beans, spaghetti, bread, pepper, and saffron; cook over medium heat for 15 minutes.

3 Meanwhile, make the pistou by whisking together the garlic, tomato paste, basil, and cheese in the bottom of a large soup tureen. Slowly beat in the olive oil. Beat 1 cup of the soup into the pistou, and then add the rest of the soup and mix well. Serve immediately.

pappa **al pomodoro** (**bread** and **tomato** soup)

THIS SOUP IS PROOF that the whole can be greater than the sum of its parts. It was taught to me by a young American cook in Florence and has been a favorite for years. You will need time, but not a great deal of concentration. It's perfect to cook in a kitchen full of chattering guests. Use the finest olive oil you can find and choose an excellent country bread — semolina if possible. This soup is also delicious at room temperature.

³/₄ cup extra-virgin olive oil
2 garlic cloves, chopped
1 large loaf day-old country bread, cut into 1-inch cubes
1 bunch fresh sage, leaves chopped and stems discarded, or 1 generous tablespoon dried sage leaves

3 pounds tomatoes, peeled and seeded, or 2 (28-ounce) cans imported crushed or puréed tomatoes
Coarse salt and freshly ground black pepper
Freshly grated Parmesan cheese

Prep/Cooking Time: 1 hour

Serves
6

1 Heat the oil in a large saucepan over medium-high heat. Briefly sauté the garlic. Add the bread and sage to the pan. Using a wooden spoon, stir until the bread turns golden brown.

2 Add the tomatoes; season with salt and pepper.

3 Bring to a boil and cook for 5 minutes, stirring constantly. Add just enough cold water to cover the tomato-bread mixture. Reduce the heat, cover, and simmer over low heat for at least 30 minutes, stirring frequently, until the bread has absorbed the tomatoes and become mushy. If the soup is too thick, add a bit of water.

4 To serve, ladle into individual bowls and garnish with grated cheese.

martha's tomato soup

THIS IS MARTHA STOREY'S TRADEMARK SOUP, which she serves at a fall gathering of campers and their families. A large pot of this fragrant mix of spices and fresh garden tomatoes dresses up simple sandwiches.

  1 large onion, chopped
  2 slices bacon, diced
 10 black peppercorns
 10 whole cloves
  2 tablespoons brown sugar
  6 cups fresh tomatoes, peeled
      and chopped (canned tomatoes
      can be substituted)

  2 tablespoons butter
  2 tablespoons all-purpose flour
  2 cups chicken or turkey stock
  1 cup half-and-half

Preparation/
Cooking Time:
30 minutes

Serves

1 Cook the onion and bacon in a Dutch oven over medium heat until the onion is translucent and the bacon is crisp. Remove all but about 1 tablespoon bacon fat.

2 Grind the peppercorns and cloves using a mortar and pestle and then add to the Dutch oven along with the brown sugar; simmer for several minutes, stirring constantly. Stir in the tomatoes and cook for 10 minutes.

3 Remove from the heat and purée in batches in a blender. Remove large pieces of cloves and peppercorns. Set the soup aside in a large bowl.

4 Make a roux in the Dutch oven by melting the butter and stirring in the flour over low heat. Cook for 1 minute and add the stock. Cook until thickened, stirring frequently.

5 Add the tomato mixture; heat, but do not boil. Swirl in the half-and-half at the last minute and serve hot.

homemade turkey soup

I GET COMPULSIVE ABOUT MAKING TURKEY SOUP because I can't bear to throw away the leftover carcass from a roast turkey. Rich turkey stock makes an excellent soup.

2 quarts turkey stock

2 cups turkey meat cut into
   1-inch chunks

2 carrots, peeled, sliced,
   and partially precooked

2 large potatoes, peeled, cut into
   $1/2$-inch chunks, and partially
   cooked in the microwave

1 teaspoon dried tarragon

1 cup washed and shredded fresh
   spinach

Salt and freshly ground black
   pepper to taste

1   Place the stock, turkey, vegetables, and tarragon in a large stockpot. Bring to a boil; reduce the heat and simmer until everything is hot, about 15 minutes.

2   Add the spinach; add salt and pepper to taste and cook for 5 minutes, or until the spinach is wilted. Serve hot.

Preparation/
Cooking Time:
20 minutes

Serves
8

TURKEY STOCK

Preparation Time: 5 hours • Makes 6–8 quarts

- 1 turkey carcass with stuffing and meat removed and reserved
- 1 onion, cut into quarters
- 1 bay leaf
- 10 black peppercorns
- 1 teaspoon salt
- 1 cup celery leaves
- 1 fresh parsley sprig

Place all ingredients in a large stockpot. Add enough water to cover the bones (8–10 quarts). Bring to a boil, cover, reduce the heat, and simmer for 5 hours.

Strain the stock and refrigerate until the fat congeals on top. Remove fat and freeze the stock in 1-quart containers until ready to use.

lentil soup

I ADD FRESH SPINACH TO MANY HOMEMADE SOUPS. Kate's friend Dee first suggested how wonderful it is in lentil soup, and she was right! Vegetarians can skip the kielbasa, though it adds a smoky layer of flavor that I personally love. You can make this soup the day before, or even weeks before, and freeze it, as long as you don't add the spinach. Save that until the soup is gently bubbling and almost ready to serve. Pop it in and simmer until it's wilted but still bright green. Swiss chard is a good alternative.

Preparation Time:
20 minutes

Cooking Time:
45 minutes

Serves

1 garlic clove, minced
½ cup chopped celery
1 onion, chopped
1 cup chopped carrot
½ pound kielbasa or other sausage
2 cups lentils, rinsed and
    picked over
1 teaspoon dried thyme
6 cups water

4 cups fresh spinach, washed
    and shredded
2 ½ cups peeled and chopped
    tomatoes, fresh or canned
1 tablespoon brown sugar
1 tablespoon lemon juice
1 tablespoon red wine vinegar
½ teaspoon salt
    Freshly ground black pepper

1 Steam the garlic, celery, onion, and carrots in 2 tablespoons water in a stockpot over low heat until the vegetables are tender, about 10 minutes.

2 Slice the sausage and brown it in a skillet. Drain and pat the sausage with paper towels to remove excess fat.

3 Add the sausage and lentils to the stockpot along with the water and thyme. Bring to a boil, turn down the heat, cover, and simmer for 30 minutes, or until the lentils are tender.

4 Uncover and add the spinach, tomatoes, brown sugar, lemon juice, vinegar, salt, and pepper; simmer for an additional 15 minutes, stirring occasionally. Serve hot.

corn **chowder**

MY MOM MADE CORN CHOWDER THIS WAY, and for me it is the gold standard, despite the many variations that I have clipped and filed over the years. This is my comfort food of choice. Sometimes I add a can of creamed corn to get a thicker texture, but mostly it is the thinner, more traditional chowder that I prefer. Bacon and cheddar cheese on top are just the perfect garnishes.

4 slices bacon
1 medium onion, chopped
1 red bell pepper, cored, seeded, and chopped
1 celery stalk, chopped
4 cups frozen yellow corn
1 teaspoon salt
$^1/_2$ teaspoon thyme
$^1/_4$ teaspoon white pepper

3 medium Yukon gold potatoes (about $^1/_2$ pound), scrubbed and cut into $^1/_2$-inch chunks
5 cups chicken broth, homemade if possible
1 cup half-and-half
1 cup grated sharp cheddar cheese (4 ounces)

Preparation Time:
20 minutes

Cooking Time:
20 minutes

Serves

1 Cook the bacon in a large stockpot over medium heat until browned and crisp. Drain on paper towels, crumble when cool, and reserve. Pour off all but 1 tablespoon of the bacon fat.

2 Add the onions to the pot and cook over medium heat for about 2 minutes, until soft and translucent. Add the bell pepper and celery and continue cooking and stirring until the onions are translucent, about 5 minutes. Add the corn, salt, thyme, and pepper, and cook for 1 minute, stirring constantly.

3 Put the potatoes in the pot, add the broth, and bring to a boil. Turn the heat down to a simmer, cover, and cook for 20 minutes, or until the potatoes are easily pierced with a fork. Stir in the half-and-half and heat gently.

4 Ladle the soup into bowls and sprinkle with the cheese and crumbled bacon.

SAND WICHES

SANDWICHES CAN BE HOT, THEY CAN BE COLD, AND THEY CAN FIT INTO THE CUISINE OF ANY SEASON.

The combinations for fillings and breads are endless, and even include lowly but lovable pb & j on squishy white bread. In summer, when cooking becomes simple and casual, and gardens and markets burst with fresh foods, what better way to make use of the bounty than to layer it between fresh, wholesome breads? In colder seasons, heat up that sandwich on a griddle for a simple supper. Sandwiches are casual eating at its best, limited only by imagination and supply.

When weekend guests are at your house, stocking up on sandwich makings is essential. You can just put out all the fixin's and let your guests build their own sandwiches at their leisure. Or, because they're the perfect portable food, you can make, wrap, and pack them and be off for your day's adventure with friends.

tomato basil sandwiches

AN ALL-TIME GREAT SUMMER SANDWICH! Tomatoes and basil are a perfect pairing that Italians have known about for generations. To get the peak experience with these few simple ingredients, farm- or garden-ripened tomatoes are a must, as is bright, fresh basil. If you are lucky enough to grow tomatoes, make the sandwiches when the tomatoes are warm from the sun and the basil leaves are just plucked from the plant.

VERSION 1

12 slices of your favorite soft
    whole-grain bread
1 (8-ounce) package light cream
    cheese (you will not use all of it)
3 medium tomatoes, thinly sliced

Salt and freshly ground
    black pepper
Handful of fresh
    basil leaves

Preparation Time:
15 minutes

Serves
6

Lay out 6 slices of bread and spread a thin layer of cream cheese on each.

Arrange tomato slices on top of the cheese and season with salt and pepper.

Cover the tomatoes with basil leaves, then top each with another slice of bread. Cut into halves and serve.

VERSION 2

12 slices Italian semolina bread
3 medium tomatoes, thinly sliced
    Salt and freshly ground
    black pepper

Handful of fresh
    basil leaves
Extra-virgin olive oil

Lay out 6 slices of bread and arrange tomato slices on top of each; season with salt and pepper.

Cover the tomatoes with basil leaves, sprinkle with olive oil, and top each with another slice of bread. Cut into halves and serve.

burgers with great toppings

MY BEST HOME-COOKED BURGER IS MADE FROM GOOD-QUALITY BEEF that is not produced in a feedlot. Top with a thick slice of garden-fresh beefsteak tomato and serve on a squishy whole wheat hamburger bun. The juiciest burgers come from 85 percent ground chuck. When we grill hamburgers, we put out an array of toppings, including, of course, ketchup and mustard, salt and pepper, sliced onions, pickles, and tomatoes. I have always added a little oregano to the ground beef before shaping the burgers.

  2 pounds ground beef
10 soft whole wheat hamburger rolls
   Dried oregano (optional)

Preparation Time:
20 minutes

Grilling Time:
10 minutes

Serves

1 Prepare a medium-hot fire in a charcoal or gas grill.

2 Shape the meat into 10 patties. Place the rolls on a platter on the table. Arrange the condiments in pretty bowls on the table.

3 Grill the burgers until cooked to the desired doneness, turning once. Toast the rolls if desired. Place the burgers on a big platter on the table and let everyone top their own.

OPTIONAL TOPPINGS:

- Sliced avocados or prepared guacamole
- Cooked bacon
- Sliced cheddar cheese
- Spread made from blue cheese, chopped walnuts, and garlic
- Slices of a creamy blue cheese

- Boston lettuce
- Sliced Vidalia or other sweet onions
- Artichoke hearts mashed with Parmesan cheese and a little mayonnaise

pan bagnat

PAN BAGNAT MEANS "BATHED BREAD" IN FRENCH and refers to the fact that the prepared sandwich is allowed to sit and "marinate" for a period of time before being served. Pan bagnat can take many forms; here, it's a Mediterranean-style chicken salad grilled inside a baguette for a delightfully satisfying summertime sandwich. As an alternative to grilling, cook the sandwich in a panini pan or on a griddle.

1 loaf French bread
1 garlic clove, crushed
Olive oil

Preparation Time:
30 minutes

Setting Time:
at least 30 minutes

Grilling Time:
15 minutes

Serves
4

DRESSING

¼ cup chopped fresh parsley
¼ cup chopped fresh basil
1 garlic clove, minced
4 anchovy fillets

2 tablespoons capers
2 tablespoons lemon juice
¼ cup olive oil

FILLING

1 medium onion, thinly sliced
½ cup sliced marinated
artichoke hearts
2 medium tomatoes, sliced
1 green or red bell pepper, roasted,
peeled, and cut into chunks

12 black olives, sliced
¼ pound thinly sliced
provolone cheese
1–2 cooked chicken breast halves,
thinly sliced

1 Cut the loaf of bread in half lengthwise; rub with crushed garlic and drizzle with olive oil.

2 To make the dressing, add the parsley, basil, garlic, anchovy, capers, and lemon juice to the bowl of a food processor with the metal blade in place and process until evenly combined. Continue processing while gradually adding the olive oil.

3 Spread the dressing on each bread half, and layer one half with slices of onion, artichoke hearts, tomatoes, peppers, olives, cheese, and chicken.

4 Put the two bread halves together and wrap tightly in aluminum foil. Set on a cutting board or baking pan and put a heavy weight on top. Chill in the refrigerator for at least 30 minutes, up to overnight.

5 Prepare a medium fire in a charcoal or gas grill.

6 Unwrap the sandwich and cut it in half. Place in a grill basket and grill until the bread browns and the cheese melts, 5 to 10 minutes per side. If you don't have a grill basket, place the two halves on the grill, brown one side, and turn carefully with two large spatulas to brown the other side. Cut each piece in half and serve.

grilled lamb pocket burgers with chopped cucumber salad

WENDY, A HOMETOWN FRIEND AND WONDERFUL COOK AND CATERER, first prepared these at a picnic on Angel Island in San Francisco Bay years ago. They are a lovely change from plain old beef burgers to cook on your backyard barbie or to take on a picnic where you know there is a grill.

Preparation Time:
20 minutes

Chilling Time:
3 hours

Grilling Time:
20 minutes

Serves

2 pounds lean ground lamb
1 egg white
½ cup finely ground fresh whole wheat breadcrumbs
2 cups crumbled feta cheese (8 ounces)
4 garlic cloves, minced
2 teaspoons dried oregano
1 tablespoon ground cumin

¼ cup chopped fresh cilantro
¼ cup chopped fresh mint
8 pita pockets (white or whole wheat)
2 medium tomatoes, sliced
1 small sweet onion, thinly sliced
Chopped Cucumber Salad (see next page for recipe)

1 Combine the lamb, egg white, breadcrumbs, half of the feta, the garlic, oregano, cumin, cilantro, and mint in a large bowl. Mix well with your hands and form into 8 patties. Refrigerate for at least 3 hours.

2 Prepare a medium fire in a charcoal or gas grill.

3 Grill the lamb burgers until they are only slightly pink inside, about 10 minutes on each side.

4 Cut the top third from each pita and insert the extra bread inside the pocket. Warm the pitas on the grill and slide the burgers into the hot pockets. Serve with the remaining feta, the tomatoes, the onions, and the Chopped Cucumber Salad.

CHOPPED CUCUMBER SALAD ✕

Preparation Time: 15 minutes • Makes 1 1/2 quarts

- 2 cucumbers, peeled and cut into 1/4-inch chunks
- 1 cup nonfat plain yogurt
- 1 tablespoon chopped fresh mint leaves
- 1 tablespoon chopped fresh cilantro leaves
- 1/2 teaspoon ground cumin

Mix all the ingredients together in a small serving bowl just before serving.

PANINI

Panini are Italian versions of sandwiches, often served hot or grilled. One birthday, my daughter Kate gave me a ridged electric panini maker, which allows me to put fresh ingredients between two slices of bread, place it quickly between two hot surfaces, and in seconds have a lovely, ridged, grilled sandwich with meltingly warm insides. I go through phases of getting it out and experimenting with different ingredient combinations. The basic method is to use good bread, place the filling between the two slices, lightly butter or oil the outsides, and cook the sandwich on a hot surface.

THESE ARE SOME OF MY FAVORITE CONCOCTIONS:

- Bitter and sweet greens and Gorgonzola cheese on multigrain bread
- Ham and cheese on rye
- Tomatoes, fresh mozzarella, and fresh basil leaves on French rolls
- Roasted red peppers with herbed goat cheese on thick slices of white country bread
- Chicken with aioli (garlic mayonnaise) and sliced olives on a horizontally sliced loaf of ciabatta
- Sliced turkey, Swiss cheese, avocado, and lettuce on whole wheat sandwich bread
- Tuna packed in olive oil, capers, and olive paste on sourdough sandwich bread
- Roast beef slices with grilled red onions, arugula, and horseradish mayonnaise

WRAPS

Instead of using bread for your sandwiches, use big flour tortillas. Place the filling in a line in the center, fold the ends over the filling, and then roll up the sandwich. As with panini, there are many ways to fill a wrap. One favorite of mine is grilled chicken with hummus and tzatziki (a Greek yogurt, garlic, and cucumber sauce). Grilled vegetables also make a wonderful filling, either by themselves or with a little grated cheese. And any kind of sliced meat and cheese with a bit of lettuce makes a great wrap.

finger sandwiches

I CAN'T IMAGINE FINGER OR TEA SANDWICHES ANYWHERE BUT AT TEA, or perhaps an old-fashioned ladies' luncheon. They must be delicate, absolutely fresh, and filled with small amounts of lusciousness. My friend Ellen and I once offered a ladies' tea and hat party as a silent auction item and found that it was wildly popular. Pots and pots of tea and trays of sandwiches were consumed as the afternoon wore on and the conversation livened.

1 loaf unsliced white bread
1 loaf unsliced whole wheat bread
2 tablespoons butter, softened
Assorted fillings

Preparation Time:
30 minutes

Serves

1 Remove the crusts from the bread and cut the loaves into thin slices. Spread a thin layer of butter on each slice of bread, add fillings of choice to one slice, top with another slice, and cut into small squares, triangles, or strips. Make some white sandwiches, some wheat, and some with a slice of each for a pretty presentation.

2 Wrap the sandwiches in plastic wrap and refrigerate until tea time.

ASSORTED FILLINGS

- Light cream cheese mixed with grated cucumber and minced fresh dill
- Sliced pickles and minced ham mixed with light cream cheese and a few drops of milk
- Peanut butter and jam
- Mashed banana and peanut butter
- Light cream cheese, thinly sliced tomatoes, and basil leaves
- Drained crushed pineapple or chutney and light cream cheese

ONE-DISH ENTRÉES

THE APPETIZING AROMA OF A SAVORY STEW SIMMERING ON THE STOVE TOP OR A FLAVOR-PACKED CASSEROLE BAKING IN THE OVEN INVITES JOYFUL ANTICIPATION OF GOOD FOOD TO FOLLOW.

When life is busy and fast-paced, entertaining should be relaxed and, well, entertaining. Our "one-dish" recipes are easy to assemble and cook ahead and will allow time and opportunity to savor a beautifully prepared meal with good company.

It is important when choosing a "one-act" meal to offer something substantial and lively enough to satisfy discerning appetites. Shop carefully for the best ingredients available so that the star of the meal will be full of flavor. We have plenty of inspiration and ideas for you, from DeeDee's ultimate one-dish meal, mac and cheese (page 118), to complex and exciting stews like Stifado (page 102) and our spicy Cajun jambalaya for a crowd (page 104). Choose a recipe, add a salad, warm crusty bread, and wine, and then sit back and enjoy the evening.

Serving directly from a stockpot kept warm on the stove allows at-ease guests the freedom to choose a favored spot to eat in front of the TV if the big game is on, or in a cozy corner where they can chat. Gathering around a table and serving family-style is another pleasant option. It offers everyone, including the cook, a chance to relax.

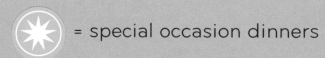 = special occasion dinners

stifado

STIFADO IS A HEARTY, SPICY GREEK STEW WITH MANY VARIATIONS. Like many regional stews and specialties, there are as many ways to make stifado as there are cooks who prepare it. It is one of the few beef stew recipes where the spatter-filled process of browning the beef is eliminated, saving time and a messy stove top. I like to use the little white boiling onions, but when pressed for time will substitute whole frozen onions, which are smaller. As with all stews, making it a day ahead improves the flavor. Add a green salad and a crusty loaf of bread, and there is your simple dinner for good friends.

1 tablespoon butter
1 tablespoon olive oil
3 pounds stewing beef, cut in
   $1/2$-inch chunks
$2 1/2$ pounds small white onions,
   peeled, or 2 pounds frozen
   pearl onions
$1/2$ teaspoon salt
$1/4$ teaspoon freshly ground
   black pepper

1 (6-ounce) can tomato paste
$1/2$ cup red wine
2 tablespoons red wine vinegar
1 tablespoon brown sugar
1 garlic clove, minced
1 bay leaf
1 cinnamon stick
$1/2$ teaspoon whole cloves
$1/4$ teaspoon ground cumin
2 tablespoons currants (optional)

Preparation Time:
30 minutes

Cooking Time:
3 hours

Serves

8

1 Heat the butter and oil in a large Dutch oven over medium heat. Add the meat and stir just to coat, but not brown. Arrange the onions over the meat. Sprinkle with salt and pepper.

2 Mix together the tomato paste, wine, vinegar, sugar, and garlic, and pour over the onions and meat. Sprinkle the bay leaf, cinnamon stick, cloves, cumin, and currants, if using, over the top.

3 Bring the stew to a boil, then reduce the heat and simmer, covered, for 3 hours, or until the meat is very tender. Do not stir the stew as it cooks, but adjust the heat so that it doesn't burn on the bottom.

4 Remove the cinnamon stick and bay leaf, stir, and serve.

NOTE: Currants are actually dried Zante grapes. Do not use fresh currants.

TIPS: • To keep the onions from falling apart, make an X in the root end of each with a sharp knife.

• If the stew bubbles while cooking, invert a heatproof plate on top of the ingredients to prevent excess movement.

MENU FOR AN APRÉS-SKI DINNER ✕

• Stifado
• Crusty sesame seed bread
• Big Green Salad (page 74) with
• Jane's Dressing (page 68)
• Dodge Bars (page 240)

steve's **jambalaya**

FOR A NEW ORLEANS TREAT, MAKE THIS SPICY CAJUN STEW, which is great for a crowd because it can be made ahead. In fact, it is better if made the day before. Parts of the meal can be frozen and put together on the day of your party. Making chicken stock from scratch adds a lovely layer of flavor, but in a pinch you can use canned chicken broth and shredded meat from a cut-up cooked chicken. Steve, a friend with a fabulous palate, learned to cook this in New Orleans and happily shared it. We have made it for 150 people, and we've also cooked it in the oven with great results. Serve it with cornbread and coleslaw for a relaxed, casual supper.

Stock-Making Time:
2 1/2 hours

Preparation Time:
45 minutes

Cooking Time:
45 minutes

Serves
12

CHICKEN STOCK

1 (4- to 5-pound) roasting chicken, cut into pieces
1 carrot, peeled and chopped
1/2 onion, chopped
3 bay leaves
1 celery top
1 teaspoon salt
8 black peppercorns

2 tablespoons canola oil
1 1/2–2 pounds andouille sausage or kielbasa, cut into 1/2-inch pieces
2 onions, chopped (about 4 cups)
3–4 celery stalks, chopped (about 2 cups)
2 green bell peppers, cored, seeded and chopped
3 garlic cloves, minced
2 tablespoons brown sugar
1 teaspoon salt
Freshly ground black pepper
5–6 cups chicken stock
1 teaspoon cayenne pepper, or to taste
4 cups brown rice
2 bunches scallions, chopped (about 1 cup)

1 To make the stock, put the chicken in a large stockpot. Add the carrot, onion, bay leaves, celery top, salt, and peppercorns, partially cover with 4 quarts of

cold water, and bring to a boil. Turn down to a simmer, partially cover, and cook for about 20 minutes, until the chicken loses its pink color. Remove the chicken from the pot and let cool until you can handle it. Pull the meat from the bones and set aside. Return the bones to the pot and simmer, covered, for 2 hours, to make the stock. Shred the chicken into 2-inch pieces and refrigerate until ready to use. Strain the stock into a large container and cool in the refrigerator. Measure out the 6 cups you will need and freeze the rest for another use. Discard the bones.

2 Heat the oil in a large Dutch oven over medium heat and sauté the sausage until brown. Remove from the pot and set aside. Add the onions, celery, peppers, and garlic to the pot and sauté until slightly wilted, about 7 minutes. Add the brown sugar, salt, and pepper and cook for another minute, until caramelized.

3 Return the chicken and sausage to the pot and cook for a few minutes to blend the flavors. Add 5 cups of the stock to the cayenne, and then the rice. Bring to a boil, stir, and reduce the heat to a simmer. Cover and cook for 35 minutes, until rice is cooked. Add the scallions and more stock, if desired, and cook for 10 minutes longer.

COOKING JAMBALAYA IN THE OVEN

After adding the stock and rice, pour the mixture into a large roasting pan and cover tightly with heavy-duty aluminum foil. Bake in a 350°F oven for 55 to 60 minutes. Check midway through cooking and add more stock if needed. Stir in the scallions after 45 minutes.

✕ VEGETARIAN JAMBALAYA

Use vegetable stock instead of chicken stock and substitute 4 large portobello mushrooms (sauté them with the vegetables) and 2 cans of drained kidney beans for the sausage and chicken.

shrimp and beef fondue with sauces

EIGHT PEOPLE IS A GOOD NUMBER TO SHARE ONE FONDUE POT. This recipe makes for a congenial, interactive meal. Give diners two long fondue forks each so that they can cook either beef or shrimp until sated. At least three different sauces provide a nice variety of dipping flavors. Try salsa, Mustard Sauce (page 157), Curry Sauce (use Mustard Sauce recipe, substituting curry powder for Dijon mustard), or the Horseradish Sauce and Spinach Dressing that follow. Friend Sandy started serving fondue on Christmas Eve to our two families, along with her wonderful cheesy rice and a simple salad. The tradition moved to California with my daughter, and now with us. We have found that with extra fondue pots, it is easily expanded to include extra relatives and friends.

Preparation Time:
30 minutes

Serves
8

1 quart peanut oil
1¹⁄₂ –2 pounds boneless beef
tenderloin, sirloin, or filet of
beef, cut into 1-inch cubes
1¹⁄₂ pounds large or jumbo shrimp,
shelled and deveined

1 At the table, pour the peanut oil into a fondue pot with sides that curve inward to avoid spattering. Heat to a temperature at which a piece of shrimp dropped in cooks quickly.

2 Arrange the raw beef on one platter and the raw shrimp on another; pass around the table. Have each person spear the food of choice and cook it in the hot oil. Be careful not to overcrowd the fondue pot, because the oil temperature will drop. Serve the sauces in small bowls on the side for dipping.

FONDUE SAUCES

HORSERADISH

- 1/2 cup light sour cream
- 1/4 cup nonfat plain yogurt
- 2 tablespoons mayonnaise
- 2 tablespoons prepared horseradish

Combine all the ingredients in a small bowl and mix well.

SPINACH

- 2 cups baby spinach leaves
- 3 tablespoons lemon juice
  Salt and freshly ground black pepper
- 1/4 cup olive oil

Combine the spinach leaves, lemon juice, and salt and pepper in a food processor until well blended.

Slowly add the olive oil and process until the sauce is blended and slightly thickened.

jezz's chili

I DON'T THINK OF CHILI AS A MAINSTAY OF ENGLISH COOKING, but Jezz, who is English, brought this delicious recipe with him when he moved to the States to marry my daughter Meg. Not only is it a great meal, but it can be put together quickly. Enlist the help of your guests with the cutting and chopping. As with many chili recipes, the quantities are not carved in stone. If you love mushrooms, add more, and include other varieties. It's hard to beat chili for casual entertaining. Most people love it, you can make it ahead, and it freezes beautifully.

Prep/Cooking Time:
1 hour

Serves

1 pound lean ground beef

1 large onion, chopped

1 (15-ounce) can whole tomatoes with juice, chopped

3 tablespoons tomato paste

1 (15-ounce) can kidney beans, rinsed and drained

8 ounces fresh white mushrooms, cut in half

1½ –2 cups mixed red, yellow, and green bell peppers cut into 1-inch chunks

2 beef bouillon cubes

1–2 tablespoons chili powder, or to taste

Dash of cayenne pepper (optional)

Salt and freshly ground black pepper

1 Sauté the beef and onions in a large stockpot over medium heat. Drain off half of the fat.

2 Add all the other ingredients to the pot. Bring to a boil, then lower the heat, cover, and simmer for 40 minutes, or until the chili thickens. Taste to be sure the flavors have blended to your liking.

thai beef red curry

THAI CURRIES OFFER MANY POSSIBILITIES. When I have leftover steak I like to use it up in this deliciously colorful dish. It is quick, easy, and expandable, and it's a great dish for a last-minute gathering of good friends.

1 tablespoon canola oil
1/2 onion, thinly sliced (about 1 cup)
1 celery stalk, chopped
1 cup fresh broccoli, cut into small pieces
1/2 of a red bell pepper, cored, seeded, and chopped
1 garlic clove, minced
1 teaspoon minced fresh gingerroot

1 1/2 pounds beef tenderloin, cut into chunks, or 2 cups leftover cooked beef
1 tablespoon lime juice
1 teaspoon fish sauce
1–2 teaspoons Thai red curry paste
1 (14-ounce) can coconut milk
10 fresh Thai basil leaves
10 fresh basil leaves
1/2 cup salted peanuts, chopped

1 Heat the oil in a wok or large skillet over medium-high heat. Add the onion, celery, broccoli, and pepper, and stir-fry for 2 to 3 minutes. Add the garlic and ginger and continue cooking for another minute or two.

2 Add the beef and cook for about 5 minutes until it loses its pink color. If using leftover beef, cook for less time. Add the lime juice, fish sauce, and curry paste, and stir to blend.

3 Lower the heat to medium, add the coconut milk, and cook for 5 minutes, until heated through. Tear or chop the basil leaves and add just before serving. Top with the peanuts.

NOTE: Thai curry pastes are found in little jars or envelopes in the Asian section of the supermarket, along with the fish sauce. While coconut milk is very high in saturated fat, I much prefer it to "lite" coconut milk, which seems watery to me.

Prep/Cooking Time: 30 minutes

Serves

4

braised **lamb** with vegetables

BIG, FULL-FLAVORED STEWS ARE THE PERFECT make-ahead meal because they only get better with reheating. With a crisp salad and a warm sourdough baguette, you have a fabulous dinner. Dress it up with fancy tableware or keep it simple. Either way, the stew will provide a warm and wonderful winter meal.

Preparation Time:
20 minutes

Cooking Time:
1 1/2 hours

Serves

3 pounds lean, boneless lamb breast and neck meat (or lamb stew meat), trimmed of fat and cut into 1-inch cubes

1/4 cup all-purpose flour

1/2 teaspoon salt

1/4 teaspoon freshly ground black pepper, plus more for seasoning

1 tablespoon canola oil

1 tablespoon sugar

4 garlic cloves, mashed

1 teaspoon dried thyme

3 large ripe tomatoes, chopped, juice and seeds reserved

3 fresh parsley sprigs, tied together with kitchen twine

1 1/2 cups hot water

4 medium potatoes, peeled and halved

2 tablespoons minced fresh parsley

1 Dredge the lamb by placing it in a paper bag with the flour, 1/4 teaspoon of the salt, and the pepper, and shaking until the chunks of lamb are thoroughly coated.

2 Heat the oil in a Dutch oven over medium heat and sauté the lamb until brown on all sides. Add the sugar and cook gently while stirring.

3 Mix the garlic, thyme, and the remaining 1/4 teaspoon salt, and add to the casserole. Cook for about 1 minute, until the garlic softens.

4 Add the tomatoes with their juice and seeds, the parsley sprigs, a few gratings of pepper, and the hot water. Bring the liquid to a boil, and then reduce the heat. Simmer very slowly for 1 hour. Taste and season with salt if needed.

5 Add the potatoes and more water if it appears dry. Continue simmering for 25 minutes, or until the meat and potatoes are tender. Sprinkle with the minced parsley and serve.

MENU FOR A COOL-WEATHER DINNER WITH COLLEAGUES

- Lemon Soup (page 83)
- Braised Lamb with Vegetables
- Overnight Baked Mashed Potatoes (page 186)
- Spinach Cucumber Salad with Lime Dressing (page 59)
- Lemon Chiffon Pie (page 200)

tana's hoppin' john with smoked turkey

EATING A BOWL OF HOPPIN' JOHN ON NEW YEAR'S DAY almost guarantees good luck for the new year — or so I have been told. This flavor-filled dish originated in the American South. Our friend Tana developed this delicious and healthy version and now serves it in the chilly Minnesota winters. Ask for a chunk of smoked turkey breast at your supermarket deli counter.

Prep/Cooking Time:
About 5 hours
start to finish,
but only about
40 minutes of
concentrated
attention

Serves

1 pound dried black-eyed peas

1½ pounds spicy turkey sausage links

¼ pound smoked turkey breast, cut into ½-inch cubes

6 cups chicken broth

1 tablespoon olive oil

1 tablespoon crushed garlic

1 onion, finely chopped

1 cup finely chopped celery

2 bay leaves

2 teaspoons red pepper flakes

1 teaspoon dried thyme

1 tablespoon dried basil

Chopped red onion

Tabasco sauce

1   Cover the black-eyed peas with water and bring to a boil; boil for 2 minutes. Remove from the heat, cover the pot, and let stand for 1 hour. Drain.

2   Slice the turkey sausage into ½-inch pieces and brown in a stockpot. Add the black-eyed peas, smoked turkey, and broth, and bring to a boil.

3   Heat the oil in a saucepan over medium-high heat. Sauté the garlic, onion, and celery for about 5 minutes, until golden, and then add to the stockpot. Add the bay leaves, red pepper, thyme, and basil. Simmer, covered, for 2 hours.

4   Uncover and simmer for 15 to 20 minutes, or until the peas are just tender and the liquid is thickened. Do not overcook or it will become mushy. Ladle into an earthenware crock and serve with chopped red onion and Tabasco sauce on the side.

red beans and rice

RED BEANS AND RICE IS A TRADITIONAL NEW ORLEANS SUPPER. It begins with the "holy trinity" of Cajun cooking — onions, green bell peppers, and celery — and here it is gussied up with spicy andouille sausage. For extra heat, you can increase the amount of cayenne.

SPICE MIX

1 teaspoon salt
1/4 teaspoon dry mustard
1/4 teaspoon dried oregano
1/4 teaspoon dried thyme

1/8 teaspoon freshly ground
   black pepper
1/8 teaspoon white pepper
   Dash of cayenne pepper

1 tablespoon canola oil
1 medium onion, chopped
1 green bell pepper, chopped
1 celery stalk chopped
2 garlic cloves, minced
1/2 pound andouille sausage or
   kielbasa, sliced and then cut
   the into half-moons

1 bay leaf
2 cups chicken broth
2 (16-ounce) cans red kidney
   beans, rinsed and drained

1 1/2 cups brown basmati rice

Preparation Time:
15 minutes

Cooking Time:
30 minutes

Serves

1 Combine all the ingredients for the spice mix in a small bowl; set aside.

2 Heat the oil in a Dutch oven over medium-high heat. Add the onion, pepper, and celery. Cook for 3 to 4 minutes, stirring often, until the onions soften and become translucent. Stir in the garlic and the spice mix and cook for another minute. Add the sausage and stir and cook for another minute. Crumble the bay leaf into the pot and add 1 cup of the broth and the beans, and bring to a boil. Cover, lower the heat, and simmer for 15 minutes. Stir in the remaining 1 cup chicken broth. Continue to cook for another 10 minutes.

3 While the beans are cooking, bring the rice and 3 cups of water to a boil in a large pot. Lower the heat, cover, and simmer for 20 to 30 minutes, or until the water is absorbed. Serve the red beans over the rice.

locro de trigo

WE ASKED MY SON-IN-LAW JEZZ ABOUT HIS FAVORITE FOODS from East Anglia, England, where he grew up. He recalled his mum's Argentina stew, for which Jan kindly provided the recipe. It's a delicious, colorful, cool-weather stew. We have not found English garlic sausage readily available, but hot Italian turkey sausage is an excellent substitute.

Preparation Time:
30 minutes

Cooking Time:
2 ½ hours

Serves
6

1 tablespoon olive oil
2 onions, chopped
1 red bell pepper, seeded
  and chopped
1½ pounds lean beef round,
  cut into 1-inch cubes
1 quart beef stock
2 teaspoons paprika
1 (16-ounce) can baby lima beans
  or butter beans, drained, or
  1 (10-ounce) package frozen
  lima beans

6 slices Canadian bacon, diced
2 garlic sausages, sliced, or spicy
  Italian turkey sausages
  ($\frac{1}{2}$–$\frac{3}{4}$ pound)
½ teaspoon salt
¼ teaspoon black pepper
1 (10-ounce) package frozen corn

1 Heat the olive oil in a Dutch oven over medium heat and sauté the onions, pepper, and beef for about 5 minutes.

2 Add the stock, paprika, and beans to the pot; bring to a boil.

3 Lightly brown the Canadian bacon and sausage in a skillet, skim off some of the fat, and add the meat to the pot. Reduce the heat; cover and simmer for 2 hours, until the meat is tender and the flavors are well blended.

4 Add the salt and pepper. Add the corn, stir, and cook for 30 minutes longer over low heat. Serve hot.

shrimp and feta casserole

AN EASY AMERICAN VERSION OF A TRADITIONAL GREEK DISH called *garides me feta*, this recipe is elegant on its own or makes a wonderful addition to a buffet.

8 ounces feta cheese

2 eggs

1 cup half-and-half

1 cup plain low-fat yogurt

1½ cups shredded Swiss cheese (6 ounces)

1 tablespoon finely chopped fresh basil, or 1 teaspoon dried

1 tablespoon finely chopped fresh oregano, or 1 teaspoon dried

⅓ cup chopped fresh parsley

3 garlic cloves, minced

8 ounces cooked angel-hair pasta

2 cups mild salsa

1 pound medium shrimp, shelled and deveined

8 ounces part-skim mozzarella, shredded (2 cups)

Preparation Time: 30 minutes

Baking Time: 30 minutes

Serves

1 Preheat the oven to 350°F. Coat the bottom and sides of an 8- by 12-inch casserole dish with vegetable cooking spray.

2 Quickly rinse the feta cheese in cold water; pat dry and crumble.

3 Thoroughly blend the eggs, milk, yogurt, feta cheese, Swiss cheese, basil, oregano, parsley, and garlic in a medium bowl.

4 Spread half of the pasta over the bottom of the casserole. Cover with the salsa, add half of the shrimp, and cover the shrimp with the remaining pasta. Pour the egg mixture evenly over the pasta. Add the remaining shrimp and sprinkle the mozzarella over top.

5 Bake for 30 minutes, until warmed through, shrimp are pink, and the cheese is melted. Let the casserole stand for 15 minutes before serving.

northern italian lasagna

LASAGNA IS NOT A QUICK AND EASY DISH TO MAKE, but this wonderful, creamy version, adapted from the classic lasagna of Bologna, is worth the time. Inspired by a recipe from a wonderful cookbook called *Private Collection* by the Junior League of Palo Alto/Mid-Peninsula California, it can be made ahead and is easily doubled.

12 lasagna noodles or 3 sheets fresh pasta
1 cup fresh breadcrumbs
1 tablespoon butter

MEAT SAUCE

1 teaspoon olive oil
1/2 pound lean ground beef
1 medium onion, chopped
3 garlic cloves, minced
2 carrots, peeled and chopped
3 ounces chopped lean ham
1/2 cup hearty red wine, such
    as Zinfandel
4 large tomatoes, seeded and
    chopped, or 4 cups canned
    chopped tomatoes

1/4 teaspoon salt
2 tablespoons minced fresh parsley
2 tablespoons chopped fresh basil,
    or 2 teaspoons dried
1 teaspoon dried oregano
    Freshly ground black pepper

Preparation Time:
1 hour

Baking Time:
30 minutes

Serves

CREAMY SAUCE

3 tablespoons butter
3 tablespoons all-purpose flour
3 cups skim milk
1 cup low-sodium chicken broth

1/4 teaspoon ground nutmeg
3/4 cup freshly grated Parmesan
    cheese

1   Cook the lasagna noodles according to the package directions. Drain and set aside until ready for use. (If using fresh pasta, omit this step.)

2   To make the meat sauce, heat the olive oil in a large stockpot over medium heat. Sauté the beef, onions, garlic, and carrots for 5 minutes, until the beef loses its pink color. Add the ham and cook for 2 minutes. Add the remaining meat sauce ingredients and bring to a boil. Lower the heat and simmer, uncovered, for 40 minutes, or until the sauce is thick.

3   While the sauce is simmering, make the creamy sauce. Melt the butter in a medium saucepan over low heat. Add the flour and cook, stirring constantly, for 1 minute. Stir in the milk and cook, stirring, until thickened. Add the chicken broth, nutmeg, and cheese, and stir until smooth. Remove from the heat and set aside.

4   Preheat the oven to 400°F. Coat a 9- by 13-inch pan with vegetable cooking spray.

5   Place a small amount of meat sauce in the bottom of the pan. Cover with a layer of noodles, 1 cup meat sauce, 1 1/3 cups creamy sauce, and 1/3 cup breadcrumbs. Repeat to make two more layers. Dot with the butter and bake, uncovered, for 30 minutes, or until bubbly. Let sit for a few minutes before cutting into squares and serving.

TO MAKE FRESH BREADCRUMBS

Tear a piece of dry bread into quarters. Turn on a blender, remove the small cover from the top, and drop the pieces into the hole with the blender running.

classic macaroni and cheese

OH, THE NUMBER OF MAC AND CHEESE RECIPES I have clipped and saved and tried is endless! In the end, the classic approach is my favorite, and this recipe is the most comforting of the comfort foods. My concession to the high fat of the cheese is to use nonfat milk. Mac and cheese is great when served from the pot, and also wonderful when baked with a topping; I give you both options here. The recipe is easily doubled to serve a larger group. Usually I just serve it with a salad, because who can say no to seconds on mac and cheese, and why have a lot of extra food hanging around?

Preparation Time:
20 minutes

Cooking Time:
25 minutes

Serves
4

10 ounces elbow macaroni
 4 tablespoons ($\frac{1}{2}$ stick) butter
$\frac{1}{4}$ cup unbleached all-purpose flour
$\frac{1}{4}$ teaspoon salt
   Freshly ground black pepper
$\frac{1}{4}$ teaspoon dry mustard
$\frac{1}{8}$ teaspoon cayenne pepper

$\frac{1}{8}$ teaspoon ground nutmeg
 2 cups nonfat milk
 2 cups grated sharp cheddar
   cheese (6 ounces)
 1 cup grated Asiago cheese
   (4 ounces)

TOPPING

 3 tablespoons whole wheat
   panko breadcrumbs
$\frac{1}{4}$ cup freshly grated Parmesan
   cheese

1 For baked macaroni and cheese, preheat the oven to 375°F. Butter a 2-quart casserole dish.

2 Cook the macaroni according to the package directions. Drain and set aside.

3 Melt the butter in a medium saucepan over medium-high heat. Stir in the flour, salt, pepper, mustard, cayenne, and nutmeg, and cook for 1 minute, or until bubbly. Whisk in the milk and cook for 5 to 7 minutes, stirring occasionally, until the mixture boils and thickens.

4 Turn the heat to low, stir in the cheddar and Asiago cheeses, and cook until they melt. Remove from the heat and serve immediately, unless you are planning to bake it.

5 For baking, combine the breadcrumbs and Parmesan cheese in a small bowl. Pour the cheese and pasta mixture into the prepared casserole dish. Evenly scatter the crumbs over the top and bake for 25 minutes, or until bubbly. Serve while hot.

MAKE-AHEAD MAC

To make the mac and cheese a day ahead, prepare the casserole except for the crumb topping. Cover with plastic wrap and refrigerate. Let the casserole sit at room temperature for 1 hour before baking. The pasta will absorb some of the sauce, so you might want to stir in an extra 1/4 cup of milk before adding the topping. Scatter the topping on just before baking.

seared sea scallops with lime chipotle cream

PLUMP, SUCCULENT SEA SCALLOPS are dotted with fresh parsley and pan-seared to a golden brown caramelized crust. The zip of smoky chipotle and tangy lime juice complete this rich, wonderful dish. Do the sauce and prep work ahead of time; searing the scallops is fast and easy.

LIME CHIPOTLE CREAM

1 scant teaspoon chipotle chile powder
Juice of 1 lime (about 2 tablespoons)
⅓ cup sour cream

Prep/Cooking Time: 15 minutes

Serves

as a main course or

as an appetizer

¼ cup olive oil
1 cup finely chopped fresh parsley
Salt and ground white pepper
2 pounds sea scallops (about 25), rinsed and patted dry

1 tablespoon finely chopped fresh chives
2 lemons, quartered

1   To make the lime chipotle cream, whisk together all the ingredients in a small bowl. Transfer the mixture to a squeeze bottle with a small tip or to a small pitcher. This step can be done up to 2 days in advance. Store the sauce in the refrigerator.

2   Heat the olive oil in a nonstick skillet over high heat until it smokes.

3   Toss the parsley with salt and pepper. Press the tops of scallops into the mixture to coat.

4 Reduce the heat to medium-high and cook the scallops in the skillet, parsley side down, for 2 to 3 minutes, until caramelized. Cook the scallops in two batches or use two pans to avoid crowding.

5 Turn and sear the bottoms of the scallops for 1 to 2 minutes. The scallops should be translucent in the center. Place on serving plates and drizzle with Lime Chipotle Cream. Sprinkle with the chives and garnish with the lemon wedges.

MENU FOR A CASUAL GRAZING DINNER

- Seared Sea Scallops with Lime Chipotle Cream
- Pinwheels (page 47)
- Asian Torte (page 43)
- Sliced Beef Tenderloin (page 138)
- Beet, Orange, and Fennel Salad with Gorgonzola and a Savory Vinaigrette (page 68)
- Mousse au Chocolat (page 223)

salmon with bowties and dill

IF YOU HAVE ANY LEFTOVER SALMON, THIS IS THE PERFECT WAY TO USE IT UP. In fact, I often cook a little extra to make sure I can prepare this lovely, savory dish.

Prep/Cooking Time:
35 minutes

Serves
4

1 tablespoon olive oil
1/2 cup minced shallots
1/2 teaspoon salt
1/4 cup white wine
2 cups chicken broth
1 cup heavy cream
1/3 cup chopped fresh dill

1 teaspoon lemon zest
1 tablespoon lemon juice
12 ounces salmon, cooked and broken into chunks (about 2 cups)
8 ounces bowtie pasta
Fresh dill sprigs for garnish

1 Heat the oil in a large skillet over medium heat. Add the shallots and cook for 2 minutes, until they begin to wilt. Sprinkle with the salt and add the wine. Cook for 1 minute, until the wine evaporates.

2 Add the broth and cream, increase the heat to medium-high, and cook for 20 minutes, stirring occasionally, until the mixture reduces somewhat. Stir in the dill, lemon zest, juice, and salmon. Cook for about 4 minutes longer, until the salmon is heated through.

3 Meanwhile, bring a large pot of salted water to a boil. Add the pasta and cook according to the package directions. Drain, add the pasta to the salmon sauce, and stir to blend completely. Serve in pasta bowls and garnish with dill sprigs.

✕ POACHING SALMON

Place uncooked salmon skin-side down in a medium skillet. Add enough water to come halfway up the salmon. Bring to a boil, cover, reduce the heat, and poach at a simmer for 3 to 4 minutes, until it just begins to flake. Remove salmon from the pan, cool, and break into 1-inch chunks.

chicken with wild rice and cherries

THIS IS MY ENTERTAINING MAINSTAY. It can be made ahead and reheated, and guests, even small ones with small appetites, almost always request seconds.

1 cup wild rice
4 tablespoons (½ stick) butter
4 tablespoons all-purpose flour
2½ cups chicken stock
8 ounces mushrooms of your
    choice, sliced (about 2 cups)
1 teaspoon lemon juice
1 tablespoon minced shallot

¼ cup half-and-half
Pinch of ground nutmeg
Salt and freshly ground
    black pepper
2 cups cooked, cubed chicken
    breast
½ cup dried cherries

1 Rinse and drain the wild rice. Place the rice in a saucepan with 2½ cups water. Bring to a boil, cover, lower the heat, and simmer for 1 hour, until tender. Drain.

2 Preheat the oven to 350°F.

3 To make the sauce, melt 3 tablespoons of the butter in a medium saucepan; add the flour, and blend. Whisk in the stock, and let simmer for 15 minutes.

4 Melt the remaining 1 tablespoon butter in a medium skillet over medium heat. Add the mushrooms and lemon juice. When the mushrooms are tender, add the shallots and continue to cook until most of the liquid has evaporated. Add the mushroom mixture to the sauce. Add the half-and-half, nutmeg, and salt and pepper. Simmer for 15 minutes longer.

5 Blend the chicken, cherries, rice, and sauce in a 9- by 13-inch casserole dish. Cover loosely with aluminum foil and bake for 45 minutes.

Preparation Time:
1½ hours

Baking Time:
45 minutes

Serves

south-of-the-border lasagna

TANA HAS TAKEN THE WONDERFUL FLAVORS OF THE SOUTHWEST with her from New Mexico to Minneapolis, where she brightens the long winters with creative, healthy cooking.

2 pounds ground turkey
1 medium onion, chopped
1 garlic clove, minced
2 tablespoons chili powder
3 cups canned or jarred
   marinara sauce
1 (4-ounce) can chopped
   green chiles

12 corn tortillas
2 cups nonfat small-curd
   cottage cheese
1 egg
2 cups grated Monterey Jack
   cheese (8 ounces)
1/2 cup grated cheddar cheese
   (2 ounces)

Preparation Time:
45 minutes

Baking Time:
30 minutes

Serves

TOPPINGS

1 cup chopped scallions
1 cup sour cream mixed with
   1/2 cup low-fat plain yogurt

1 cup sliced black olives

1 Preheat the oven to 350°F.

2 Brown the meat in a large skillet over medium heat. Add the onions and garlic and cook until tender. Sprinkle with chili powder, and mix well.

3 Stir in the tomato sauce and green chiles; simmer over medium heat for 15 minutes. While the mixture simmers, dip the tortillas in it to soften them. Remove and set aside.

4 Beat together the cottage cheese and egg and set aside.

5 In a 9- by 13-inch casserole, spread a layer of one-third of the meat mixture. Top with a layer of half of the Jack cheese, then half of the cottage cheese, and then half of the tortillas. Repeat this process, ending with a layer of meat sauce. Top with the grated cheddar.

6 Bake for 30 minutes. Place the toppings in individual bowls and serve on the side.

MENU FOR A SOUTHWEST DINNER ✕

- South-of-the-Border Lasagna
- Spinach Cucumber Salad with Lime Dressing (page 59)
- Coffee frozen yogurt
- Salsa de Chocolate (page 237)

chili blanco

THIS WHITE CHILI IS LIGHT IN COLOR but bold in flavor, and it's a snap to prepare. Serve it in an earthenware casserole surrounded by an assortment of mixed or matched small bowls heaped with the colorful garnishes. And don't forget the cornbread!

3 (20-ounce) cans cannellini
   beans, rinsed and drained
1 (13-ounce) can low-salt
   chicken broth
1 tablespoon extra-virgin olive oil
2 large garlic cloves, minced
2 cups chopped onions
1 jalapeño pepper, seeded
   and minced

1 (4-ounce) can chopped
   green chiles
2 teaspoons ground cumin
2 teaspoons dried oregano
1/4 teaspoon ground cinnamon
   Hot pepper sauce
2 cooked whole chicken breasts,
   cut into small cubes
   (about 4 cups)

Preparation Time:
45 minutes

Cooking Time:
15 minutes

Serves

1 Combine the beans with the chicken stock in a stockpot and heat gently over low heat while you prepare the other ingredients.

2 Heat the oil in a small skillet over medium-high heat. Sauté the garlic until light brown; add the onions and cook until soft. Remove from the heat and blend in the peppers and seasonings.

3 Toss the chicken cubes with the onion mixture and add to the beans. Mix gently. Heat, but don't allow to boil, over medium heat for 10 to 15 minutes.

SUGGESTED GARNISHES:
• Sliced black olives
• Chopped plum tomatoes
• Chopped scallions
  (green part only)

• Shredded light cheddar cheese
• Mix of half sour cream and half
  low-fat plain yogurt

GIRL TALK MENU

THREE BOOK GROUP DINNERS

- Shrimp and Feta Casserole (page 115)
- Bibb lettuce with Jeanne's Salad Dressing (page 75)
- Judy Mac's Strawberry Dessert (page 228)

- Zucchini Bisque (page 79)
- Greek Shrimp Salad (page 62)
- Tender little rolls
- Individual Lemon Pudding Cakes (page 220)

- Dilled Mustard-Baked Salmon (page 158)
- Green Beans with Toasted Pine Nut Oil (page 171)
- Hot and Cold Sesame Noodles (page 183)
- Lemon Chiffon Pie (page 200)

TWO AFTERNOON TEAS

- Assorted Finger Sandwiches (page 99)
- Meg's Scones (page 21)
- Clotted cream (look in specialty food shops)
- Light Lemon Bars (page 234)
- English tea with milk and sugar

- Sliced smoked salmon with Yogurt Spread (page 34), capers, and sliced red onions
- Rye crackers and bagel chips
- Iced tea, Fresh Lemonade (page 248), and chilled Champagne

LATE, LAZY SUNDAY AFTERNOON GET-TOGETHER

- Brie and Pear Pizza (page 44)
- Spinach and Arugula Salad with Strawberries and Orange Dressing (page 58)
- Lemon Poppy Muffins (page 25)
- Wine spritzers

lemon **chicken** and **vegetable** kabobs

YOU CAN'T MISS WHEN PUTTING LEMON AND CHICKEN TOGETHER. Add some herbs, fresh vegetables, and a grill, and you have a perfect summer dinner. Most of the work is done ahead of time so that you can enjoy your guests while dinner is grilling. Toss some fresh corn on the grill to complete the meal. When we lived in New England, we would go up the hill to the farm stand just before dinner, choose warm ears that had just been picked, and husk and cook them — sometimes in boiling water, sometimes on the grill.

Preparation Time:
20 minutes

Marinating Time:
1–2 hours

Grilling Time:
30 minutes

Serves

MARINADE

¼ cup canola oil
½ cup lemon juice
½ teaspoon salt
2 teaspoons dried marjoram
2 teaspoons dried thyme

1 teaspoon freshly ground
black pepper
2–3 garlic cloves, minced
1 small onion, chopped
½ cup chopped fresh parsley

KABOBS

3 whole chicken breasts, boned,
skinned, and cut into
1-inch chunks
3 small zucchini, cut into
½-inch slices

2 cups cherry tomatoes
2 Vidalia onions, thickly sliced
½ pound white mushrooms,
cut in half
10–16 skewers

1 Mix all the marinade ingredients together in a small bowl. Put the chicken chunks into a medium bowl and pour three-quarters of the marinade over them. Stir to coat all the pieces.

2 Put all the vegetables into a large bowl, pour the remainder of the marinade over them, and mix gently. Cover the chicken and the vegetables and refrigerate for 1 to 2 hours.

3 Prepare a hot fire in a charcoal or gas grill.

4 Thread the chicken onto skewers, leaving about $1/8$-inch spaces between the chunks. Arrange the vegetables in a colorful manner on skewers. Save the veggie marinade to use on leftovers; discard the chicken marinade.

5 Carefully lay the chicken skewers on the hot grill. Cook for about 5 minutes; turn and cook for another 5 minutes, or until the chicken is firm to the touch. Cut into one to check for doneness.

6 Add the vegetable skewers to the grill once the chicken is done. Cook for 5 minutes, or until they begin to brown and soften, but don't let them get mushy. Serve hot. If you have any leftover vegetables, put them back in the marinade; store in the refrigerator and serve as a salad.

NOTE: If you use bamboo skewers, soak them in water for at least 1 hour before grilling.

build-your-own
tostadas with chicken

A FAVORITE QUICK SUPPER, TOSTADAS OFFER GREAT VARIETY in a light, healthy meal. Unlike a taco, where the tortilla is folded and filled, a tostada is built on a flat tortilla, stacked with good things. The quantities in this recipe are just a guide; feel free to adjust them to fit the number, tastes, and appetites of your guests.

Preparation Time:
20 minutes

Serves
6

4–8 flour tortillas (depending on appetites)
1 cup Black Bean Dip (page 32)
3 medium tomatoes, chopped (about 1 cup)
1 whole cooked chicken breast, shredded
1–2 cups shredded jalapeño Jack cheese, cheddar, or any other highly meltable cheese (4 to 8 ounces)

1 can chopped green chiles
1 cup nonfat plain yogurt
1½ cups Kate's Fresh Salsa (page 33) or use bottled salsa
2–4 cups shredded lettuce
Chopped green bell pepper, chopped onion, or anything else that you would like to add (optional)

1 Heat a cast-iron skillet or griddle over medium heat. Soften each tortilla on the griddle for 1 minute on each side.

2 Heat the bean dip in the skillet; add 1 cup of the chopped tomatoes, and warm the entire mixture, stirring frequently.

3 Spread each tortilla with 2 tablespoons of the beans and some chicken; top with about ¼ cup shredded cheese. Heat in a microwave on High for 30 seconds, or in a 350°F oven for 5 minutes.

4 Arrange the tostadas on a platter; serve surrounded by bowls filled with the remaining tomatoes, the chiles, yogurt, salsa, and other toppings. (I like to use an assortment of handmade pottery bowls.)

5 To complete the assembly, set a tostada on a plate and sprinkle with shredded lettuce, then tomatoes, then chiles. Top with a dollop of yogurt and a spoonful of salsa. These are best eaten with a knife and fork.

MENU FOR A KID-FRIENDLY MEXICAN DINNER ✕

- **Build-Your-Own Tostadas with Chicken**
- **Black Bean Dip (page 32) and**

Kate's Fresh Salsa (page 33) with tortilla chips
- **Fresh fruit**

chip's fajitas

WHEN WENDY AND CHIP ENTERTAIN CASUAL DINNER GUESTS for the first time, this is what they serve. As their growing kids start to invite hungry teens, the meal remains a winner. The fajitas are so good that we don't care if Chip never tries anything else.

Preparation Time:
30 minutes

Marinating Time:
4 hours

Grilling Time:
20–25 minutes

Serves

Juice of 6 limes
³/₄ cup olive oil
¹/₂ cup red wine vinegar
¹/₂ cup chopped fresh cilantro
3 garlic cloves, minced
¹/₂ teaspoon red pepper flakes
2 (4-ounce) cans chopped green chiles
2 pounds boneless skinless chicken breasts

1 Spanish onion, sliced
2 red bell peppers, thinly sliced lengthwise
1 green bell pepper, thinly sliced lengthwise
1 yellow bell pepper, thinly sliced lengthwise
6 large flour tortillas
Accompaniments (see next page)

1 Combine the lime juice, olive oil, and vinegar in a medium bowl. Whisk in the cilantro, garlic, red pepper flakes, and chiles.

2 Place the chicken in a large bowl. Top with several onion slices and scatter some pepper slices evenly over the onions. Carefully pour about 2 cups of the marinade over all. Cover with plastic wrap and refrigerate for 2 hours. Put the rest of the onions and peppers in a small bowl, cover with the remaining marinade, and refrigerate.

3 After 2 hours, toss the chicken and return to the refrigerator to marinate for another 2 hours.

4 Prepare a hot fire in a charcoal or gas grill.

5 Remove the chicken from the marinade and discard the marinade. Place the chicken on the grill. Pour the onion-pepper marinade into a foil pan and place the pan on the grill. Grill the chicken, turning two or three times and basting with the vegetable marinade until thoroughly done (20–25 minutes).

6 Preheat the oven to 325°F. Wrap the tortillas in aluminum foil and warm in the oven for about 6 minutes.

7 Remove the chicken from grill and slice. Arrange on a warm platter. With a slotted spoon, remove the peppers and onions from the hot marinade and arrange in a bowl. Place the warm tortillas in a napkin-lined basket.

8 Set out the chicken, peppers and onions, tortillas, and accompaniments. Invite guests to assemble their own fajitas by putting chicken, onions and peppers, and the accompaniments of their choice on a tortilla and folding it like a taco.

ACCOMPANIMENTS

- ½ cup prepared guacamole
- 1 cup shredded Monterey Jack cheese (4 ounces)
- ½ cup low-fat sour cream mixed with ½ cup low-fat plain yogurt

make-your-own pizza

FEEL FREE TO MAKE LOTS OF DOUGH HERE, as the extra will keep very well in the freezer. It's great to be able to grab a hunk of dough from the freezer, thaw and roll it, and create toppings from whatever is in the pantry or refrigerator at the time. People of all ages love pizza and can join in the fun of preparation. Pam's sister Pat started offering pizza on Sunday night to any children and grandchildren who were around. When we moved to California and had family nearby, we instituted Sunday pizza night, and, while we sometimes order out, my favorite dinner involves making this recipe. It is the simplest of entertaining. The menu is pizza, maybe a salad, and ice cream for dessert.

Preparation Time:
30 minutes

Baking Time:
10–20 minutes

Makes

2

12-inch pizzas

4

8-inch pizzas

10

4-inch pizzas

DOUGH

1 tablespoon active dry yeast

1 cup warm water

1 teaspoon sugar

$^1/_2$ teaspoon salt

2 tablespoons olive oil

2 cups all-purpose flour

$^1/_2$ cup whole wheat flour

1 tablespoon cornmeal

Toppings (see next page)

1 To make the dough, dissolve the yeast in the warm water in a large bowl. Stir in the sugar, salt, oil, and flours. Beat the dough vigorously with a wooden spoon for 20 strokes.

2 Scrape the dough onto a floured counter and knead it until smooth.

3 Let the dough rest for 5 minutes before rolling it out. This is an important step because it allows the dough to relax, making it easier to roll.

4 For two pizzas, divide the dough in half; roll each half into a 12-inch circle on a floured surface. Lift the dough onto a baking sheet or pizza pan sprinkled with 1 tablespoon cornmeal.

5 Preheat the oven to 475°F.

6 Spread your favorite toppings on the waiting pizza dough. Bake for 10 to 20 minutes, depending on the size, or until the dough is lightly browned and the cheese is melted. Serve hot.

TOPPINGS

- Plain canned tomato sauce
- Dried oregano
- Dried or fresh chopped basil
- Pesto
- Red pepper flakes
- Grated part-skim mozzarella, or a combination of Gruyère and cheddar cheeses
- Freshly grated Parmesan cheese
- Crumbled feta cheese
- Crumbled goat cheese
- Chopped steamed broccoli
- Sliced canned artichoke hearts
- Thinly sliced green bell pepper
- Thinly sliced onion
- Peeled and sliced fresh tomatoes
- Sliced mushrooms of your choice
- Pepperoni
- Sausage
- Grilled chicken
- Anything else that appeals to you

ENTRÉES

WHEN PLANNING A MENU FOR ENTERTAINING, THE MAIN COURSE IS WHERE I START. THE CHOICE MAY BE BASED ON THE SEASON, WHAT IS ON SALE, OR JUST WHAT I FEEL LIKE COOKING.

Each spring, a friend gets an itch to make a wonderful lamb stew and then invite friends over to share it. In summer, grilling is appealing. In winter I like to have the oven on for a big hunk of meat.

In this chapter there are entrées of all sorts: beef, pork, lamb, fish, chicken, and pasta. There are a few "put on the dawg" dinners, so that you can plan ahead and have fabulous food for special guests on a special occasion. Other times, you just feel like getting together with friends at the last minute and want to throw a simple supper together. And sometimes you end up doing something in between the two. Here are recipes for any occasion.

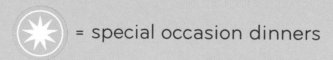 = special occasion dinners

sliced **beef** tenderloin

THE TENDERLOIN OF BEEF IS AS GOOD AS IT GETS. It is moist, velvety, and sublimely tender. While it is expensive, it is easy to prepare and serve and is the ultimate special occasion treat. The addition of white peppercorns enhances the beef's mild flavor. You won't need leftover suggestions for this one.

Parchment paper
2 tablespoons coarsely ground
white peppercorns
1 beef tenderloin, trimmed (about
4 pounds after trimming)

Preparation Time:
15 minutes

Cooking Time:
About 45 minutes
for rare, longer
for well done

Serves

1 Preheat the oven to 425°F.

2 Line the bottom of a 9- by 13-inch baking dish with parchment paper. Sprinkle with 1 tablespoon of the ground pepper. Tuck the tail under the meat and place in the dish. Press the remaining pepper into the top surface of the meat.

3 Roast the meat until an instant-read thermometer inserted into the thickest part registers 130°F (about 45 minutes). Cool slightly, and if desired, wrap whole and refrigerate to chill.

4 Fifteen minutes before serving, carve the meat into $\frac{1}{2}$-inch-thick slices.

vince's mother's italian meatballs

MY BROTHER-IN-LAW, VINCE, HAS NEVER READ A COOKBOOK, yet he is an awesome cook. He learned from watching his mother, who prepared fine Italian meals that kept family and friends at the table. His delicious meatballs are the ultimate comfort food and are a favorite throughout our circle of family and friends. Most supermarkets sell a meatloaf mixture (freshly ground veal, beef, and pork) that is perfect for these meatballs.

2 pounds ground meat mixture
(combination of veal, beef,
and pork)

1 small loaf day-old Italian bread
or medium sub roll

1 cup packed fresh parsley leaves,
tough stems removed

4 eggs

1 cup freshly grated
Parmesan cheese

Salt and freshly ground
black pepper

¼ cup peanut oil or canola oil
for frying

¼ cup olive oil for frying

Prep/Cooking Time:
40 minutes

Makes about
30
medium
meatballs

1 Blend the meat mixture with a fork in a large bowl.

2 Wet the bread and squeeze out most of the water; break into large pieces. Place the bread in a large food processor bowl and, using the metal blade, combine it with the parsley and eggs. Don't process much — just enough to chop the parsley and blend the ingredients. Add the bread mixture to the meat and, using a fork, blend thoroughly. Blend in the cheese and salt and pepper. Form into meatballs roughly the size of golf balls in the palms of your hands.

3 Heat the combined oils in a large skillet over medium-high heat. Cook the meatballs in the hot oil for about 5 minutes per side, turning only once, until they are thoroughly brown. Remove from the pan and drain on paper towels. The meatballs can then be simmered in tomato sauce or eaten plain.

rolled and stuffed flank steak

FOR ELEGANCE THAT WILL SATISFY BEEF LOVERS, look no further than this dish. Flank steak is not only an easy cut of beef to handle but also superbly flavorful. Add some creamy blue cheese and a pinch of thyme and you are well on the way to creating a fabulous meal. If there is a butcher around, ask him to pound the steak for you, otherwise, do it at home. This makes it thinner, more uniform, and more tender. It is difficult to find large flank steaks, so if you want to double the recipe, buy a second flank steak. Instead of blue cheese, you could stuff the flank steak with herbed chèvre.

$1^1/_2$ pounds flank steak, pounded until thin
$^1/_2$ teaspoon dried thyme
$^1/_2$ teaspoon salt
Freshly ground black pepper

3–4 ounces creamy blue cheese, such as blue Castello
$^1/_4$ cup whole wheat breadcrumbs
4 feet white cotton string
Olive oil

Preparation Time:
20 minutes

Roasting Time:
30 minutes

Serves
4

1 Preheat the oven to 350°F.

2 Lay the steak flat on a cutting board. Sprinkle with the thyme, salt, and pepper.

3 Mash together the cheese and breadcrumbs in a small bowl. Spread the mixture lengthwise down the center of the steak. Fold one long side over the cheese mixture and roll up the steak tightly, tucking in the ends to cover the cheese.

4 Tie the string around one end of the steak, move the string down the steak about 2 inches, wrap it around the steak, and loop the end through to create a right angle. Continue down the length of the steak until you reach the other end and it is neatly tied up. Or simply tie several shorter lengths of string around the steak every 2 inches.

5 Heat a large ovenproof skillet over medium-high heat. Rub the steak with olive oil and brown on all sides, about 3 minutes.

6 Roast for 30 to 35 minutes, or until an instant-read thermometer registers 140°F. Let rest for 10 minutes, then cut the string, slice the steak into 1-inch-thick slices, arrange on a platter, and serve.

POUNDING STEAK

To pound the flank steak, use a small meat-tenderizing mallet, available in kitchenware stores. Or use a wide, heavy-bottomed tumbler. The purpose is to break the tissue slightly and make it more tender and, in this case, to make the piece of flank steak thinner and of uniform thickness.

MENU FOR AN ELEGANT DINNER FOR EIGHT

- Pomegranate Cocktail (page 249)
- Hot Crab Dip (page 39)
- Apple Pumpkin Soup (page 78) served in espresso cups
- Rolled and Stuffed Flank Steak
- Creamed Spinach (page 173)
- Bread basket
- Pear, Pecan, and Blue Cheese Salad (page 71)
- Mousse au Chocolat (page 223)

pasta with chunky tomato **mushroom** sauce

THIS SAUCE can handle any sturdy pasta shape you throw at it.

1 tablespoon olive oil

2 cups sliced portobello
    mushrooms

1–2 garlic cloves, minced

1 (8-ounce) can plain tomato sauce

1 (28-ounce) can plum tomatoes,
    coarsely chopped

Salt and freshly ground
    black pepper

1/4 cup chopped fresh basil, or
    2 teaspoons basil purée

1/2 cup freshly grated Parmesan
    cheese (2 ounces)

1 pound pasta of your choice

Prep/Cooking Time:
40 minutes

Serves

1 Heat the olive oil in a large skillet over medium heat and sauté the mushrooms for 5 to 10 minutes. Add the garlic and sauté a few minutes longer.

2 Add the tomato sauce and tomatoes. Season with salt and pepper and basil. Cook for 20 minutes over medium heat, until the sauce has thickened. Stir in the Parmesan.

3 Meanwhile, bring a large pot of salted water to a boil and cook the pasta. Drain well, pour into a large serving bowl, and pour the sauce over it.

summer **spaghetti**

WHEN THE TOMATOES ARE RIPE and the weather is hot, you will love this fresh-tasting spaghetti dinner. The hot spaghetti melts the cheese, and then the flavors of summer take over.

1 pound spaghetti
Olive oil (enough to coat
   the pasta)
1/3 pound part-skim mozzarella or
   other cheese, cut into 1/4-inch
   cubes
6–8 pitted black olives, cut in half
1 garlic clove, minced
3 ripe tomatoes, cut into
   bite-size chunks

Handful of fresh basil leaves,
   chopped
2 tablespoons minced fresh
   parsley
Dash of red pepper flakes
1/2 teaspoon dried oregano
Salt and freshly ground
   black pepper

1 Bring a large pot of salted water to a boil and cook the pasta al dente. Drain and toss with olive oil.

2 Meanwhile, prepare the sauce in a large serving bowl by combining all of the remaining ingredients.

3 When the pasta is done, pour it on top of the sauce and let it sit for a few minutes. Toss and serve immediately.

Preparation Time:
30 minutes

Serves

saté babi

OUR OLD FRIEND JEAN SHARED THIS WONDERFUL RECIPE with us years ago. Now, with carefully trimmed, vacuum-packed pork tenderloins easily available, we have revived this old standby.

1 teaspoon ground coriander
1 teaspoon ground cumin
1/2 cup light soy sauce
1/2 cup light or dark brown sugar
1/2 cup canola oil

3 pounds pork tenderloin, cut into 2-inch cubes
3 large onions, cut into 2-inch chunks
Skewers

Preparation Time:
15 minutes

Marinating Time:
Overnight

Grilling Time:
About 20 minutes

Serves
6–8

1 Mix together the coriander, cumin, soy sauce, brown sugar, and canola oil in a large bowl. Add the pork and onions, stir to mix, and marinate overnight in the refrigerator.

2 Prepare a hot fire in a charcoal or gas grill. Alternate pork and onion chunks on skewers.

3 Grill the skewers for about 20 minutes, until the pork is cooked through, rotating every 5 minutes.

MENU FOR A MIDSUMMER BACKYARD BARBECUE

- Saté Babi
- Creamy Crunchy Potato Bake (page 184)
- Sliced tomatoes with chopped fresh basil, extra-virgin olive oil, and balsamic vinegar
- Raspberry sherbet and vanilla ice cream with blueberries

tuscan **pork** tenderloin

THE FLAVORS AND AROMAS OF TUSCANY — ROSEMARY, SAGE, GARLIC — and salt blend perfectly with pork. Wrapping them together in a baguette makes a sensational presentation. I learned about this dish at Judy Witts's cooking school (La Divina Cucina) overlooking the San Lorenzo market in Florence, Italy, where we bought all the ingredients. This same method could be used for turkey breast, salmon, or beef. Serve it with green beans and a pear and gorgonzola salad.

3 fresh rosemary sprigs	2 pork tenderloins (about
12 fresh sage leaves	12 ounces each)
3 garlic cloves, peeled	Olive oil
1 tablespoon sea salt	1 medium-width 12-inch baguette

1 Remove the leaves from the rosemary sprigs and lay on a large cutting board. Chop in the sage leaves and garlic. Mince finely, then mix in the salt until thoroughly blended. Set the seasoning mixture aside in a small bowl.

2 Heat a large skillet over medium heat. Rub the pork with olive oil and brown it on all sides, about 3 minutes.

3 Trim the baguette to make it the same length as the tenderloin. Slice the baguette in half horizontally and scrape out some of the soft insides. Brush the bread halves with more olive oil.

4 Scatter some of the seasoning mixture on each bread half and rub the rest on the pork. Place the pork on one piece of bread and cover with the other. Wrap it all in aluminum foil and seal. At this point, you can store in the refrigerator for up to 24 hours until ready to cook. Let sit at room temperature for 45 minutes before cooking.

5 Preheat the oven to 350°F. Roast for 35 to 45 minutes, or until an instant-read thermometer reads 150 to 155°F. Remove from the oven, unwrap, and let rest for 5 minutes before slicing into 1-inch-thick slices.

Preparation Time:
10 minutes

Cooking Time:
40–50 minutes

Serves
4

grilled orange pork tenderloin

PORK TENDERLOIN IS ONE OF THE EASIEST, tastiest, and most adaptable pieces of pork for entertaining, and just plain eating. With no bones and no fuss, it is ready for marinating, or rubbing, or whatever you choose to do with it. This is one of the simplest ways to prepare tenderloin. Make a simple marinade with marmalade and rosemary and pour it over the meat, and it is ready to grill in minutes. Grill some vegetables alongside the tenderloin, add a rice dish or some type of potato, and you are ready with a simple, yummy meal.

$\frac{1}{4}$ cup orange marmalade
1 fresh rosemary sprig, chopped,
    or $\frac{1}{2}$ teaspoon dried rosemary
$\frac{1}{4}$ cup white wine vinegar
1 teaspoon orange zest

2 pork tenderloins (about
    12 ounces each), trimmed
    of fat and membrane
Olive oil
Salt and freshly ground
    black pepper

Preparation Time:
20 minutes

Grilling Time:
10 minutes

Serves

1 Combine the marmalade, rosemary, vinegar, and orange zest in a small saucepan; heat until the marmalade dissolves and the mixture is well blended. Reserve 2 tablespoons; pour the remainder over the tenderloins and let sit for 15 minutes.

2 Prepare a hot fire in a charcoal or gas grill and brush the rack lightly with oil.

3 Grill the tenderloins for 3 to 5 minutes per side, until the outside is brown and the inside is just barely cooked through, 150°F on an instant-read thermometer. Remove from the grill and brush with the reserved marinade. Season with salt and pepper. (The meat will continue to cook for a few minutes after it is removed from the grill.)

4 Slice the tenderloins into $\frac{1}{2}$-inch-thick slices and arrange on a large platter.

tandoori chicken

IF YOU HAVEN'T TRIED THIS SPICY INDIAN YOGURT MARINADE, you are in for a treat. An added bonus is that much of the work is done ahead. In India this dish would be cooked over coals in a tulip-shaped clay oven called a tandoor, but baking it in the oven works well. Serve it with brown basmati rice, red lentils, cucumber raita, and naan for a fabulous blend of flavors and textures. Mango chutney is also a nice accompaniment to Indian food.

1 medium onion, chopped
6 garlic cloves, minced
3 tablespoons grated fresh
   gingerroot
3 tablespoons lime juice
1 1/2 cups plain nonfat yogurt
1 tablespoon ground coriander
1 teaspoon ground cumin
1 teaspoon ground turmeric
1 teaspoon garam masala
   (optional; available in
   specialty shops)

1/4 teaspoon ground nutmeg
1/4 teaspoon ground cinnamon
1 teaspoon salt
1/4 teaspoon freshly ground
   black pepper
1/4 teaspoon ground cayenne
   pepper
2 tablespoons olive oil
8 bone-in chicken pieces
   (about 3 pounds)
1 lime, cut into wedges

Preparation Time:
20 minutes

Marinating Time:
24 hours

Cooking Time:
60 minutes

Serves

1 Mix the onion, garlic, ginger, and lime juice together in a large bowl. Add the yogurt, spices, and oil, and stir well. Remove the skin from the chicken; slash the chicken pieces diagonally three times, rinse, and pat dry. Add the chicken to the marinade and massage the marinade into the pieces. Cover and refrigerate for 24 hours, turning several times.

2 Preheat the oven to 400°F. Remove the chicken from the marinade and arrange on a rack in a large roasting pan. Spoon the marinade over the top and bake for 45 to 60 minutes, or until very tender. Serve the chicken on a large platter surrounded by lime wedges.

brined balsamic-glazed pork chops

THE HUMBLE PORK CHOP CAN BE A PERFECT SIMPLE ENTRÉE if not overcooked and dry as leather. Brining, a simple step that takes just a little advance planning, helps tremendously in terms of adding flavor and moisture. Sugar in the brining mix cuts down on the saltiness.

Chilling Time:
1–2 hours

Cooking Time:
15 minutes

Serves
6

BRINE MIXTURE

3/4 cup kosher salt
3/4 cup light or dark brown sugar
1 cup boiling water
4 crushed garlic cloves

2 bay leaves
1 tablespoon black peppercorns
4 cups cold water

PORK CHOPS

6 boneless pork chops
   (1- to 1 1/2-inches thick)
1 tablespoon olive oil
1 teaspoon salt

Freshly ground black pepper
2 tablespoons chopped shallots
1/4 cup balsamic vinegar
4 fresh sage leaves, chopped

1 To make the brine mixture, stir the salt, sugar, and boiling water together in a large stainless steel bowl until the sugar and salt are dissolved. Add the spices and cold water.

2 Pour brine into a gallon-size zipper-top plastic bag and add the pork chops. Refrigerate for 1 to 2 hours.

3 Remove the pork chops from the brine and pat dry. You may store them in the refrigerator, lightly covered, for several hours, until ready to cook.

4 Preheat the oven to 425°F.

5 Heat the oil in a large oven-proof skillet over high heat. Season the chops with the salt and pepper and place in the skillet. Brown for 1 minute on each side.

6 Transfer the skillet to the oven and bake for 8 to 10 minutes, turning once, until an instant-read thermometer registers 140°F. The chops will be a little squishy to the touch and pinkish inside. Remove from the oven and place the chops on a serving platter covered with aluminum foil, where they will continue to cook.

7 Meanwhile, return the skillet to the stove top over medium heat. Add the shallots and cook for 1 minute. Pour in the vinegar to deglaze the pan and stir up the brown bits. Cook for another minute and then add the sage. Return the chops and their accumulated juices to the pan and move around until they are just coated. Arrange them on the platter, drizzle the glaze on top, and serve. The chops will be juicy and tender and perhaps a little pink.

MENU TO CELEBRATE THE FALL HARVEST ✕

- **Blue Cheese Avocado Dip (page 33)**
- **Brined Balsamic-Glazed Pork Chops**
- **Roasted Brussels Sprouts (page 175)**
- **Gingered Carrots (page 167)**
- **Apple Walnut Cobbler (page 222)**

mustard-grilled butterflied lamb

BE SURE TO GET A GOOD PIECE OF LAMB and you will have a marvelous meal. The lamb sits in the lovely blend of marinade flavors for a day or so, and then the lamb is grilled to create a lovely, crusty, caramelized surface. Serve with simple broiled red potatoes and a julienne of summer vegetables.

Preparation Time:
30 minutes

Marinating Time:
2–3 days

Grilling Time:
30 minutes

Serves

1 tablespoon dry mustard
1 tablespoon Dijon mustard
1 teaspoon sugar
3 tablespoons water
2 large garlic cloves, mashed
1/2 cup olive oil, plus more for the grill rack
2 dried red chile peppers, broken in half and sautéed briefly in 1 tablespoon olive oil
1/2 cup loosely packed fresh rosemary leaves, finely chopped, or 2 tablespoons dried

1/4 cup lemon juice
1 teaspoon freshly ground black pepper
1/2 teaspoon salt
2 teaspoons dried oregano
1/4 cup red wine vinegar
1 (4- to 5-pound) whole leg of lamb, boned and butterflied

1 Mix all the ingredients except the lamb together in a medium bowl to make the marinade, and let sit for about 15 minutes.

2 Remove excess fat from the lamb. Pierce the meat all over with a fork. Pour the marinade into a large, shallow roasting pan. Add the lamb, massage the marinade into the meat, and cover with plastic wrap. Refrigerate the lamb for up to 2 days, turning occasionally.

3 One hour before grilling, remove the lamb from the marinade and pat partially dry.

4 Prepare a hot fire in a charcoal or gas grill and brush the rack lightly with oil.

5 Grill the lamb for 10 to 15 minutes per side until done to your liking (it should be slightly pink on the inside), 130°F for medium. Brush with the marinade a few times (but not during the last few minutes of cooking), and have a spray bottle of water handy in case the olive oil ignites.

6 Slice the lamb and arrange on a platter; sprinkle with salt and pepper and serve.

MENU FOR A SUMMER BARBECUE ✕

- Mustard-Grilled Butterflied Lamb
- Broiled Potatoes (page 190)
- Fresh corn on the cob
- Broccoli Cashew Salad (page 70)
- Julienne of Summer Vegetables (page 169)
- Plum Crisp (page 217)

roasted **rosemary** chicken

BILL AND J.B. PREPARE THIS SIMPLE AND SUPERB DISH. It will fill your kitchen with a wonderful, warm aroma that will welcome weary travelers. Roast two chickens to feed six people and have leftovers for sandwiches.

1 roasting chicken (4 to 5 pounds)
Salt
3 garlic cloves, 1 sliced into slivers
    and 2 left whole

8 fresh rosemary sprigs
2 lemons

Preparation Time:
20 minutes

Roasting Time:
1–1½ hours

Serves

4

1 Preheat the oven to 400°F.

2 Thoroughly wash and dry the chicken; rub salt inside the chest cavity. Rub the garlic on the outside and inside the chicken. Slip thin slivers of one of the garlic cloves under the chicken skin; drop the remaining two cloves into the cavity.

3 Rub the entire chicken with 3 rosemary sprigs, inside and out. Slip one sprig under the skin of each breast and place 3 of the remaining sprigs in the cavity.

4 Split one of the lemons and squeeze the juice over the inside and outside of the chicken. Place the squeezed halves in the cavity.

5 Truss the chicken and place on a rack in a roasting pan. Roast the chicken, basting occasionally, until done and the juices run clear (1 to 1½ hours).

6 Let cool to room temperature and serve garnished with the second lemon (sliced) and the remaining 2 rosemary sprigs.

grilled and chilled orange chicken

CHICKEN THIGHS ARE WONDERFUL FOR A BUFFET because they are relatively small, have a nice serving of meat on their bones, and come in quite uniform sizes. Orange and mint provide a nice brightness to the flavor of this chilled chicken. Serve it with colorful coleslaw and barley salad for a meal that is best made a day ahead. Everything can be served cold or at room temperature. The chicken is also delicious served hot.

MARINADE

2 tablespoons orange zest
Juice of 3 oranges (about 1 cup)
1/2 teaspoon ground cumin
3 garlic cloves, mashed

1/4 cup chopped fresh cilantro
2 tablespoons chopped fresh mint
2 tablespoons sesame oil
1/4 cup rice vinegar

CHICKEN

4 pounds chicken thighs
(12 pieces), skin removed, or a
combination of thighs and legs

1 orange, thinly sliced
Fresh cilantro sprigs

Preparation Time:
30 minutes

Marinating Time:
Overnight

Cooking Time:
20–30 minutes

Chilling Time:
2 hours

Serves

1 Whisk together the marinade ingredients in a medium bowl. Pour marinade over the chicken. Cover and refrigerate overnight.

2 Prepare a low fire in a charcoal or gas grill.

3 Remove the chicken from the marinade and discard the marinade. Grill the chicken for 20 to 30 minutes, turning several times, until the outsides are golden brown and the insides are cooked through.

4 Arrange the chicken on a platter, garnish with the orange and cilantro, cover with plastic wrap, and refrigerate until chilled.

herb-roasted turkey breast

A FAIRLY SIMPLE WAY TO PROVIDE A LIGHT SUPPER is to roast a whole turkey breast, which can also be used for sandwiches the next day. Serve it buffet style, thinly sliced. If you like, roast it a day ahead and serve it cold. In either case, serve with Cranberry Salsa. It's a great meal for guests, and wonderful to cook when friends are spending the weekend with you. Save the bones and make turkey stock to use in soups.

Preparation Time:
15 minutes

Baking Time:
2 1/2 hours

Serves

12

1 bone-in turkey breast
(about 5 pounds)
2 tablespoons butter
1 tablespoon dried tarragon,
plus more for sprinkling

CRANBERRY SALSA
2 large oranges
2 cups chopped cranberries
(if frozen, thaw first)
1 tablespoon finely chopped
scallions
1/4 cup olive oil

1 tablespoon dried oregano,
plus more for sprinkling
1/2 teaspoon salt
Freshly ground black pepper
1 medium onion

1 tablespoon minced fresh cilantro
1 tablespoon minced fresh
gingerroot
1 small jalapeño chile pepper,
seeded and minced

1 Preheat the oven to 325°F.

2 Rinse the turkey with cold water and pat dry.

3 Combine the butter, tarragon, oregano, salt, and pepper in a small bowl to form a paste. Spread the paste over the outside of the turkey.

4 Lay the onion in the cavity with a few sprinkles of the herbs; center the breast on a rack in a shallow roasting pan. Roast for about 2 $\frac{1}{2}$ hours, or until an instant-read thermometer registers 185°F. Baste occasionally.

5 Set the turkey on a large cutting board. Let rest for 10 minutes, then slice and arrange on a serving platter.

6 To make the cranberry salsa, grate 4 teaspoons orange zest from the oranges; place in a large bowl. Remove the remaining peel and white membranes, coarsely chop the oranges, and let the orange pieces drain in a colander.

7 Toss the cranberries with the zest. Add the chopped oranges, scallions, oil, cilantro, ginger, and jalapeño. Toss to blend. Serve, or cover and refrigerate.

MENU FOR A CHRISTMAS OPEN HOUSE ✕

- Christmas Wassail (page 244) and Strawberry Party Punch (page 245)
- Spinach Dip (page 31) with fresh vegetables
- Pesto Torte (page 35)
- Little Dogs with Currant Mustard Sauce (page 36)
- Roast turkey breast or baked Virginia ham
- Gravlax with Mustard Dill Sauce (page 38)

- Cheese board with red and green seedless grapes
- Fruitcake (page 256)
- German Christmas Bread (page 252)
- Cinnamon Stars (page 267)
- Peppermint Punch (page 246)
- Hazelnut-flavored coffee

citrus-grilled tuna

THE FRESH MARINADE here is wonderful with any grilled fish.

1 cup grapefruit juice

1 cup orange juice

$1/4$ cup lime juice

$1/2$ cup light soy sauce

1 tablespoon chopped fresh
    thyme leaves, or 1 teaspoon
    dried

$1/4$ teaspoon cayenne pepper

3 pounds tuna steaks

Olive oil

Lemon and lime slices
    for garnish

Preparation Time:
15 minutes

Marinating Time:
6 hours

Grilling Time:
15 minutes

Serves

1 Whisk together the juices, soy sauce, thyme, and cayenne in a medium bowl. Place the tuna steaks in a shallow baking dish. Pour the marinade over the fish and refrigerate for 6 hours, turning once after 3 hours.

2 Prepare a medium fire in a charcoal or gas grill and lightly oil the rack.

3 Remove the tuna from the marinade and place on the grill. Turn after about 7 minutes and continue grilling until the fish is opaque (about another 7 minutes). Place the fish on a warm platter and garnish with lemon and lime slices. Serve immediately.

grilled salmon

SIMPLE BUT ELEGANT, SALMON ADDS CLASS TO ANY MEAL. Serve it with steamed fresh green beans and Hot and Cold Sesame Noodles (page 183). Cook extra and serve it cold with the mustard sauce as an appetizer for another meal. Salmon is a wonderful, adaptable food that can take on many flavors. Season it with dill, parsley, or summer savory. Try sesame oil, soy, and other Asian flavors. If possible, use wild salmon.

1 1/2 **pounds salmon fillets**
Good-quality olive oil
1/4 **cup fresh tarragon leaves,**
plus a few sprigs for garnish
Mustard Sauce (recipe follows)

1 Rub the salmon fillets with olive oil and sprinkle with the tarragon leaves.

2 Prepare a medium fire in a charcoal or gas grill.

3 Grill the salmon for 4 to 5 minutes per side. Turn gently, as it becomes fragile when cooked. The salmon can be slightly translucent in the center when removed because it will continue to cook after it's taken from the grill.

4 Cut the salmon into serving pieces and arrange on a platter. Pour the mustard sauce over or around and garnish with a few tarragon sprigs.

Preparation Time:
5 minutes

Grilling Time:
10 minutes

Serves

6-8

MUSTARD SAUCE

- **2 tablespoons light mayonnaise**
- 1/2 **cup nonfat plain yogurt**
- 1/4 **cup Dijon mustard**
- **1 tablespoon lemon juice**
- **1 tablespoon minced fresh dill**

Mix all of the ingredients together in a small bowl. This sauce is good served with either hot or cold salmon.

dilled mustard-baked salmon

MUSTARD AND DILL AGAIN FOR SALMON, but since it is such a great combination, who can complain? This is a perfect main course for a company dinner because the preparation is done ahead, and it is simple, yet fabulous. Coating the salmon with dilled mustard keeps the fish moist and succulent while cooking. I once bought a whole Pacific king salmon off the fishing boat, and Meg prepared it this way for a Mother's Day family dinner. We all agreed it was the best salmon we had ever eaten. I strongly suggest buying fresh wild salmon for this. Serve with roasted asparagus and a citrus salad. If any salmon is left, it makes a wonderful cold lunch.

Preparation Time:
5 minutes

Cooking Time:
20 minutes

Serves

1 tablespoon olive oil
2 ½ pounds salmon fillets, washed
  and cut into 8 pieces
1 cup panko breadcrumbs, whole
  wheat if available
1 teaspoon salt

Freshly ground black pepper
1 garlic clove, minced
¼ cup chopped fresh dill,
  plus sprigs for garnish
¼ cup Dijon mustard
Lemon wedges for garnish

1 Preheat the oven to 350°F. Brush olive oil on both sides of the salmon and place the pieces in a large roasting pan.

2 Combine the breadcrumbs, salt, pepper, and garlic in a small bowl. Mix the dill and mustard together in another small bowl and brush on the fillets. Sprinkle the crumb mixture on top and press into the mustard coating.

3 Bake the salmon until the crust is slightly brown and the fish just cooked through, 15 to 20 minutes. Carefully lift the fillets out of the pan with two spatulas, leaving the skin behind.

4 Arrange on a platter with the dill sprigs and lemon wedges.

poached white fish with tomatoes and fennel

EXCEPT FOR THE TIME I TILTED MY LARGE SAUTÉ PAN after serving this lovely dish, splattering the remaining tomato sauce all over my white kitchen cabinets, this dish has never failed me. There are many kinds of white fish one can use. In Massachusetts, my favorite was cod loins; on the West Coast, I use ling cod or halibut. Thai basil's slightly anise flavor intensifies the fennel nicely. If you can't find it, use regular basil.

1 tablespoon olive oil
1 small fennel bulb, chopped
   (about 1¼ cups)
½ cup minced shallots
2 garlic cloves, chopped
1 (28-ounce) can whole tomatoes,
   chopped

1 teaspoon orange zest
½ teaspoon salt
   Freshly ground black pepper
1 bay leaf
6 (6-ounce) cod or halibut fillets
   (about ¾ inch thick)
1 fresh Thai basil sprig, chopped

Prep/Cooking Time:
45 minutes

Serves

1 Heat the olive oil in a large skillet over medium heat. Add the fennel and shallots and cook for about 10 minutes, or until the vegetables are soft and translucent. Add the garlic and cook for another minute, stirring.

2 Add the tomatoes, orange zest, salt, pepper, and bay leaf. Bring to a boil, then lower the heat, partially cover, and simmer for about 15 minutes.

3 Nestle the fish fillets in the sauce, spooning sauce over them. Cover and continue cooking for 10 to 12 minutes, or until the fish is flaky. Serve garnished with the basil.

NOTE: An alternative is to make the sauce ahead, then pour it into a shallow casserole dish, add the fish, cover with aluminum foil, and bake at 350°F for 15 to 20 minutes.

stir-fried shrimp with glazed walnuts

A FRIEND BROUGHT THIS TO A POTLUCK SUPPER, and many of us asked him for the recipe. Later I had it as part of a Chinese banquet. On occasions, I couldn't get enough. It demonstrates the fusion of Eastern and Western cooking and the creativity of the Chinese cooks in Hong Kong by using mayonnaise in the sauce. Accompany these shrimp with rice and braised greens or stir-fried vegetables.

Marinating Time:
30 minutes

Cooking Time:
5 minutes

Serves

1 tablespoon dry sherry or rice wine
1 tablespoon cornstarch
1 teaspoon salt
   Freshly ground black pepper
1 pound large shrimp, shelled,
   cleaned, butterflied, and
   patted dry

$^1/_3$ cup mayonnaise
2 tablespoons chicken broth
1 teaspoon sugar
1 tablespoon lemon zest
1 teaspoon sesame oil
1 tablespoon canola oil

GLAZED WALNUTS

1 cup walnut halves
$^1/_2$ cup sugar
$^1/_4$ cup water
$^1/_4$ teaspoon salt

$^1/_2$ teaspoon ground cinnamon
$^1/_2$ teaspoon vanilla extract

1   Mix together the sherry, cornstarch, $^1/_2$ teaspoon of the salt, and the pepper in a medium bowl. Add the shrimp and let marinate for 30 minutes.

2   Combine the mayonnaise, broth, sugar, lemon zest, sesame oil, and the remaining $^1/_2$ teaspoon salt in a small bowl and set the sauce aside.

3 To make the glazed walnuts, preheat the oven to 350°F. Place a cooling rack over a sheet of wax paper (for draining the walnuts).

4 Put the walnuts on a baking sheet and toast for 3 minutes, until they become lightly browned and fragrant. Set aside.

5 Bring the sugar, water, salt, and cinnamon to a boil in a small saucepan over medium heat. Continue cooking, without stirring, until the mixture reaches 236°F on a candy thermometer. (This is the soft-ball stage, which means that a drop of the mixture will form a soft, squishy ball in a cup of cold water.) Remove from the heat and beat with a wooden spoon until it begins to look creamy. Add the walnuts and vanilla extract and stir to combine. Cool the walnuts on the prepared rack, separating them with a skewer or fork while still hot.

6 To cook the shrimp, heat the canola oil in a wok or large skillet over high heat. Drain the shrimp and stir-fry for a minute or two, until they begin to curl up and turn pink. Add the sauce and cook for 1 minute, until the sauce heats through and thickens slightly. Place in a serving bowl, scatter the walnuts on top, and serve.

lemon catfish

FARM-RAISED CATFISH IS A POPULAR DISH IN THE SOUTH. There is even an annual catfish festival in Belzoni, Mississippi. For many in the rest of the United States, this mild and delicate fish is little known at best, and considered a garbage fish at worst. One wonderful meal I was served in the South included crispy, deep-fried catfish and fried hush puppies. Catfish is also delectable cooked gently with subtle seasoning.

8 catfish fillets (about 2 pounds)
1/4 cup fresh lemon juice
2 tablespoons all-purpose flour
1/4 teaspoon salt
1/4 teaspoon freshly ground
    white pepper

1 teaspoon butter
1 teaspoon olive oil
1/4 cup minced fresh parsley
1 lemon, cut into quarters

Preparation Time:
10 minutes

Cooking Time:
5–10 minutes

Serves
8

1 Rinse the fillets and pat dry. Pour the lemon juice into a shallow baking dish.

2 Mix the flour, salt, and pepper together on a plate. Dip the fillets in the lemon juice and then turn them in the flour mixture to coat.

3 Melt the butter and oil together in a large nonstick skillet over medium-high heat. Quickly sauté the fish until the flesh is opaque and the outside lightly browned, about 2 minutes per side.

4 Transfer the catfish to a platter, sprinkle with the parsley, and arrange the lemon wedges on the side.

lime-grilled halibut

HALIBUT IS A NICE, FIRM-FLESHED FISH THAT GRILLS WELL. It has a lot of fat under the skin that can cause the grill to flare up, so have some water in a spray bottle on hand. Use a fish basket if you have one; otherwise use two large spatulas for turning the fish. The citrusy brightness of lime combined with the salty depth of soy sauce and the richness of the fish makes for an opulently flavored dish.

2 1/2 pounds halibut steaks

MARINADE

1/2 cup lime juice

1/4 cup olive oil

1/4 cup soy sauce

2 garlic cloves, mashed

1/4 cup chopped fresh basil

Freshly ground black pepper

2 limes, cut into wedges

Fresh basil leaves

Preparation Time:
15 minutes

Marinating Time:
30 minutes

Grilling Time:
15 minutes

Serves

1 Rinse the fish steaks and pat dry; place in a shallow nonmetallic dish.

2 Mix together the marinade ingredients and pour over the steaks. Cover with plastic wrap and refrigerate for 30 minutes.

3 Prepare a hot fire in a charcoal or gas grill. Remove the fish from the refrigerator.

4 Grill the fish for 5 to 10 minutes per side (depending on thickness), or until the flesh is opaque. Arrange the fish on a platter and garnish with the lime wedges and basil leaves.

SIDE DISHES

MAIN DISHES BECOME SENSATIONAL MEALS WHEN THE VEGETABLES AND GRAINS ARE PERFECTLY MATCHED.

Bread and tossed salad go with practically everything, but there are so many other possibilities. Potatoes are a great standby with meats, and you will find many choices here. Colorful vegetables are a must for texture, interest, and, of course, nutrition. If we are trying to create a rainbow on our plates, we must have vegetables. Think of ginger-glazed carrots (page 167), balsamic Brussels sprouts flavored with bacon (page 175), roasted asparagus (page 180), ratatouille for the height of summer (page 166), and more. Our selection of side dishes includes plenty of colorful vegetable sides, and just as many substantial sides featuring grains and potatoes.

ratatouille

THIS OPULENT DISH IS ACTUALLY EASIER TO PREPARE than the classic recipe, which calls for sautéing some of the vegetables. It is best prepared a day in advance. Leftovers are delicious served with crumbled goat cheese in a pita pocket. For a colorful dish, use red and yellow peppers instead of green.

1 medium eggplant
Salt
1 large onion, chopped
2 green bell peppers, seeded and thinly sliced
2 medium or 4 small zucchini, diced
6 medium tomatoes, peeled, seeded, and diced
2 large garlic cloves, crushed

Freshly ground black pepper
1 tablespoon sugar
1 tablespoon red wine vinegar
1 tablespoon dried oregano
1 teaspoon dried marjoram
3 tablespoons extra-virgin olive oil
$1/2$ cup water
25 pitted black olives (optional)
$1/4$ cup finely chopped fresh basil
$1/4$ cup finely chopped fresh parsley

Preparation Time:
20 minutes
plus 1 hour for
draining eggplant

Cooking Time:
1 hour and 15 minutes

Serves

6-8

1 Cut the eggplant in half lengthwise. Slash the cut surface and sprinkle it with salt. Lay the eggplant, cut side down, on paper towels for 1 hour to drain out the bitter water. Cut into $1/2$-inch cubes.

2 Gently toss together all of the ingredients except the oil, water, olives, basil, and parsley in a large pot. Add the olive oil and the water, cover, and cook slowly over low heat until tender, about 1 hour.

3 Uncover and cook for another 10 minutes to reduce the liquid. Stir in the olives if using, basil, and parsley, and cook 5 minutes longer. Remove from the heat and let cool slightly. Serve warm or at room temperature.

glazed gingered carrots

COOKING CARROTS BRINGS OUT THEIR SWEETNESS and, for an added bonus, helps release the good nutrients. They are a highly neglected but wonderful vegetable. This very simple side dish adds color, flavor, and healthy goodness to chicken, fish, or any kind of meat.

1 pound carrots, peeled and cut
  into ¼-inch disks
¼ cup water
2 tablespoons butter
½ cup minced shallots

1 teaspoon grated fresh gingerroot
1 teaspoon brown sugar
  Salt and freshly ground
    black pepper

1 Cook the carrots in a microwave-safe dish with the water for 5 minutes on High. Let sit for 5 minutes, until the carrots are easily pierced with a fork.

2 Meanwhile, melt the butter in a medium skillet over medium-high heat. Quickly cook the shallots for 1 or 2 minutes, until translucent. Add the ginger and carrots and cook another 2 minutes. Add the brown sugar and cook until it melts. Season with salt and pepper and serve.

Prep/Cooking Time:
20 minutes

Serves

grilled summer **vegetables**

GRILLING VEGETABLES IS EASY, and it preserves nutrients and enhances flavor. It is a great way to add color to the meal as well. Select bright, fresh vegetables and wash them carefully before slicing. Use a vegetable grill pan, which will prevent the smaller vegetables from falling though the cracks. Grilled vegetables are wonderful with any meat or fish that you cook on the grill. Try them with a pork tenderloin and polenta.

6 cups assorted sliced vegetables:
    eggplant, zucchini, pattypan
    squash, red onions and
    sweet onions (cut into thick
    slices lengthwise), bell peppers,
    fennel, radicchio, asparagus,
    carrots, green beans, or
    whatever you have on hand

4 tablespoons chopped fresh thyme
    leaves, or 1 tablespoon dried
Salt and freshly ground
    black pepper

Prep/Cooking Time:
20 minutes

Serves

6

1 Prepare a hot fire in a charcoal or gas grill.

2 Brush the grill rack with extra-virgin olive oil, lay the vegetables on the grates, and cook for a few minutes on each side, until they are browned and slightly tender. Sprinkle with the thyme.

3 Arrange the vegetables on a platter and season with salt and pepper. Drizzle with several tablespoons of olive oil and serve.

INDOOR GRILLING

If you have a ridged grill pan or griddle, you can cook the vegetables on the stove top for about 5 minutes, turning them when they get brown ridges on one side.

julienne of summer vegetables

WHILE CUTTING VEGETABLES INTO MATCHSTICKS is time-consuming (unless you have a mandoline), the result is delightful. Lightly steaming them brings out the color and tenderizes them just enough. The smooth, simple Asian dressing is a nice touch. Serve this colorful dish as an alternative to tossed salad any time of year

4 cups assorted vegetables cut into 2 $\frac{1}{2}$- by $\frac{1}{8}$-inch julienned sticks: carrots, zucchini, parsnips, kohlrabi, scallions, and any other vegetable that suits your taste

1 garlic clove, minced

1 tablespoon soy sauce

$\frac{1}{4}$ cup chicken broth

2 tablespoons dry white wine

1 tablespoon rice vinegar

1 teaspoon cornstarch

Salt and freshly ground black pepper

Prep/Cooking Time:
30 minutes

Sitting Time:
1 hour

Serves

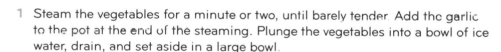

1 Steam the vegetables for a minute or two, until barely tender. Add the garlic to the pot at the end of the steaming. Plunge the vegetables into a bowl of ice water, drain, and set aside in a large bowl.

2 Mix the soy sauce, broth, wine, vinegar, and cornstarch in a small saucepan. Cook over low heat until the sauce boils. Pour over the vegetables and let sit for at least 1 hour. Season with salt and pepper and serve at room temperature.

red lentils

KATE INTRODUCED US TO THE WONDERFUL, SPICY FLAVOR OF RED LENTILS, which became a staple of her graduate school existence. They're a great accompaniment to Tandoori Chicken (page 147), and also make a delicious meatless meal with basmati rice, chutney, and Cucumber Raita (page 55). Kate always heats the spices, as Indian cooks do. I don't always take the time but know that doing it enriches the flavor of the spices.

2 teaspoons canola oil
1/2 teaspoon whole cumin seeds
1 garlic clove, minced
1 tablespoon grated fresh
   gingerroot
1/2 teaspoon ground cinnamon
1/4 teaspoon ground cloves
1/4 teaspoon ground cardamom

1/4–1/2 teaspoon cayenne pepper
1 medium onion, chopped
1 1/4 cups red lentils, rinsed
   and drained
1 teaspoon ground turmeric
1/2 teaspoon salt
2 1/2 cups water

Prep/Cooking Time:
30 minutes

Serves

1 Heat the oil over medium heat in a large saucepan. Add the cumin seeds and heat them until they pop. Add the garlic, ginger, cinnamon, cloves, cardamom, cayenne, onion, and lentils. Cook until the onion is translucent.

2 Add the turmeric, salt, and water; bring to a boil. Turn down the heat and simmer, uncovered, until much of the water has evaporated as the lentils bubble slowly, stirring occasionally. This will take about 15 minutes. Serve hot.

green beans with toasted pine nut oil

MY DAUGHTER-IN-LAW, CATHERINE, IS AN INSPIRED COOK. She is part of a talented dinner group that researches, plans, creates, and serves exciting and challenging meals fit for royalty. This is Catherine's recipe, a wonderfully simple, fresh, and flavorful side dish, and, as her note on the recipe says, "always a winner."

3 **pounds whole fresh green beans, ends trimmed**
1 cup pine nuts, lightly toasted
6 tablespoons olive oil
   Salt and freshly ground black pepper

Prep/Cooking Time: 15 minutes

Serves

1 Bring a large pot of salted water to a boil. Add the beans and cook until firm but tender, about 3 minutes after the water returns to a boil. Drain, rinse with cold water, drain well, and transfer to a large bowl.

2 Coarsely grind the pine nuts in a food processor. Transfer to a medium bowl and mix in the oil. Add the mixture to the beans and toss to coat. Season to taste with salt and pepper.

NOTE: Both the beans and the pine nut oil can be prepared a day ahead. Cover the cooked beans and refrigerate. Store the oil mixture, covered, at room temperature. Let the beans stand at room temperature for 1 hour before tossing with the oil and serving.

sautéed broccoli and garlic

FRESH BROCCOLI IS GOOD FOR SO MANY REASONS, not the least of which are the bright color and fresh crunch that come from light steaming — the simplest way to prepare it. But I can get bored with that and also find that it can turn a nasty wilted greenish brown or become cold very fast. Enter sautéed broccoli and garlic. Do the steaming early in the day and sauté the garlic ahead of time. Just before serving, toss the broccoli in the pan, sauté it quickly with the garlic, and serve warm, adding the essence of garlic while keeping the color and crunch of broccoli.

1 bunch broccoli, trimmed,
   stems peeled, and cut into
   3-inch pieces
1 tablespoon olive oil
3 garlic cloves, thinly sliced

Prep/Cooking Time:
20 minutes

Serves

1 Steam the broccoli over rapidly boiling water for 5 to 10 minutes, or until the broccoli is tender-crisp and easily pierced with a knife. Rinse with very cold water and drain well. At this point, you can store the broccoli in a plastic bag in the refrigerator until ready to sauté.

2 Heat the olive oil in a large skillet over medium heat and quickly sauté the garlic until golden brown. Add the broccoli and stir-fry until the broccoli is heated and garlic and oil are distributed throughout. Serve immediately.

sautéed spinach

THE PEOPLE OF FLORENCE, ITALY, LOVE SPINACH, and any time a menu includes the word "Florentine," you can be sure that this wonderfully tasty, healthy green will make an appearance. When I lived in Florence for a short time, I was thrilled to find that I could buy a ball of cooked spinach in the grocery store, which could be sautéed, creamed, and added to anything. Back home, I went to my friends Sam and Elizabeth's organic farm in the fall. After the spinach crop was harvested, I could go into the field and gather the small, very curly, tender leaves that were the last gasp of the plant. This was without doubt the best spinach I have ever eaten in any form.

**1 pound fresh spinach, trimmed
    and washed, but not dried
1 tablespoon olive oil
2 garlic cloves, minced**

**Pinch of nutmeg
Salt and freshly ground
    black pepper**

Prep/Cooking Time:
10 minutes

Serves

4

1   Place the spinach in a large skillet over medium-high heat. Cook and stir until it completely wilts and whatever water that was on it evaporates. Remove it to a cutting board and coarsely chop it. Squeeze out any excess water.

2   Wipe out the skillet and add the olive oil and garlic. Cook over medium heat for 1 minute, and then stir in the spinach. Season with nutmeg and salt and pepper, while cooking for another minute. Serve hot.

✕ CREAMED SPINACH

To make creamed spinach, proceed as above, except use butter instead of olive oil and then sprinkle 1 tablespoon flour over the spinach in step 2. Cook for 1 minute, then add ¼ cup heavy cream. Cook and stir until the cream thickens slightly, then serve.

special onion rice

OUR FRIEND SANDY MAKES THIS WONDERFULLY TASTY RICE and serves it with beef and shrimp fondue on Christmas Eve. We love it! It also has a nice, make-it-in-advance quality. Don't be surprised by the unconventional cooking method. The large quantity of onion supplies all the liquid necessary to puff the grains.

2 tablespoons butter

2 pounds onions (about 6 large onions), sliced

4 quarts water with $\frac{1}{2}$ teaspoon salt added

2 cups short-grain brown rice

$\frac{1}{2}$ teaspoon salt

$\frac{1}{4}$ teaspoon freshly ground black pepper

$\frac{1}{4}$ cup half-and-half or evaporated skimmed milk, warmed

1 cup grated Swiss cheese (4 ounces)

Preparation Time:
30 minutes

Baking Time:
1 hour

Serves

10

1 Preheat the oven to 300°F.

2 Melt the butter in a large sauté pan over low heat. Stir in the onions and cook until they are completely coated with the butter.

3 Bring the salted water to a rapid boil in a large pot; add the rice and boil for 5 minutes to soften the grain. Drain the rice and put it in a large casserole dish. Add the onions to the dish, along with the salt and pepper, and stir until well blended. Cover and bake for 1 hour.

4 Remove from the oven and let cool slightly. Add warmed half-and-half and the cheese. Stir and serve.

NOTE: To make this ahead, cool and refrigerate the casserole after step 3. Before serving, add $\frac{1}{2}$ cup water and reheat the rice over low heat. When hot, add the warmed half-and-half and cheese; stir.

roasted balsamic brussels sprouts with red onions and bacon

FRESH BRUSSELS SPROUTS ARE WONDERFUL, BUT SEASONAL. In this recipe you can use either fresh or frozen. Bacon provides a smoky complement to the pungent sprouts, sweetened by the caramelized red onion. It is a perfect dish to go with pork or turkey.

1 pound frozen or fresh
    Brussels sprouts
½ medium red onion,
    thinly sliced
2 garlic cloves, minced
1 tablespoon olive oil

3 slices meaty bacon
2 tablespoons balsamic vinegar
1 teaspoon Dijon mustard
½ teaspoon dried thyme
    Salt and freshly ground
    black pepper

Prep/Cooking Time:
15 minutes
for frozen,
30 minutes
for fresh

Serves

1   Preheat the oven to 425°F.

2   If using frozen sprouts, follow the package directions to cook them, reducing the time by half so that they are undercooked. Set aside. If using fresh sprouts, trim bottoms, cut in half, place in a roasting pan, and toss with the onions, garlic, and oil; roast for 20 minutes.

3   Meanwhile, cook the bacon until it is crisp. Drain and crumble. Whisk together the vinegar, mustard, and thyme in a small bowl.

4   If using frozen sprouts, combine them with the onions, garlic, oil, bacon, and vinegar mixture in a roasting pan and roast for 10 minutes. If using fresh, add the bacon and vinegar mixture to the sprouts and onions in the pan and roast for another 10 minutes. Season with salt and pepper and serve hot.

grilled sweet corn

BOILED FRESH CORN IS GREAT, BUT GRILLING GIVES IT A SLIGHTLY SMOKY FLAVOR. There are many ways to grill corn; this one is simple and foolproof. The main thing is to get fresh corn in season. My husband's grandfather, who lived to be 96, claimed to eat an ear every day. I can't say it contributed to his longevity, nor does it say much about his willingness to try new foods. I just think that fresh corn is something to look forward to in the summer. Buy it, shuck it, cook it, and eat it. Or, in this case, shuck it after cooking. In summer, sometimes we have just ears of corn for dinner.

12 ears fresh corn in their husks

Preparation Time:
5 minutes

Soaking Time:
1 hour

Cooking Time:
10 minutes

Serves
6

1 Pull back the husks, remove the silk, and put the husks back on the corn. Soak the corn in a large kettle of cold water for 1 hour.

2 Meanwhile, prepare a hot fire in a charcoal or gas grill.

3 Grill the corn for about 10 minutes, until the husks become browned on all sides. Remove from the grill, remove the husks, and serve with your favorite seasonings.

baked **parsnips**

THE PARSNIP IS A FORGOTTEN VEGETABLE THAT NEEDS SOME PROMOTION. We jokingly call it a "yucky" vegetable, meaning those winter root vegetables that many people ignore. Parsnips look like pale carrots, but have a much sweeter taste. Steam, mash, and serve with butter, salt, and pepper for a simple but delightful side dish. This baked version is fabulous with roast turkey breast or chicken.

1 pound parsnips (about 8), peeled, cut in half, and sliced lengthwise into equal-size pieces
$^1/_2$ cup milk

$^1/_2$ cup grated cheddar cheese (2 ounces)
$^1/_2$ cup chopped fresh parsley
1 teaspoon butter

Preparation Time:
20 minutes

Baking Time:
30 minutes

Serves

1 Preheat the oven to 325°F.

2 Steam the parsnips until tender-crisp, 5 to 8 minutes. Arrange in a shallow casserole dish coated with vegetable cooking spray.

3 Mix the milk, cheese, and parsley together; pour over the parsnips and dot with the butter. Cover with aluminum foil and bake for 30 minutes. Serve warm.

golden harvest vegetables

LIKE THE BAKED PARSNIPS ON THE PREVIOUS PAGE, this is a prime "yucky" vegetable recipe. It has been a favorite on our Thanksgiving table for years. The colorful medley of root vegetables is packed with flavor and nutrition. They can be cut and cooked in advance, then reheated and glazed just before serving.

1 pound carrots
1 pound parsnips
1 pound rutabagas

GLAZE

3 tablespoons butter
2 tablespoons lemon juice
2 tablespoons maple syrup or
   brown sugar

¹/₄ teaspoon ground cinnamon
¹/₂ teaspoon salt
   Freshly ground black pepper

Preparation Time:
35 minutes

Cooking Time
About 8 minutes

Serves

12

1 Peel and cut all the vegetables into 3- by ¹/₄-inch sticks. Steam them until tender-crisp, about 8 minutes for the carrots and rutabagas, less for the parsnips.

2 To make the glaze, warm the butter, lemon juice, maple syrup, cinnamon, salt, and pepper in a small saucepan over low heat, stirring until well blended.

3 Pour the glaze over the hot vegetables; toss gently and serve.

curried brussels sprouts and cauliflower

THIS IS A DELIGHTFUL WAY TO INDULGE in those healthy cruciferous vegetables. The dish can be prepped ahead and then cooked along with roast meat or poultry. With the fresh Brussels sprouts available in the market these days, it seems that everyone I talk to loves them. I sure do, and while this version takes some time, the result is superb.

1½ pounds Brussels sprouts,
    or 2 (10-ounce) frozen
    packages
1 head cauliflower, trimmed and
    cut into 1-inch florets
Up to 2 cups low-fat milk
2 tablespoons cornstarch
¼ cup half-and-half

2 teaspoons curry powder
1 cup light sour cream, nonfat
    plain yogurt, or a combination
    of the two
1 tablespoon butter
Salt and freshly ground
    black pepper

Preparation Time:
30 minutes

Baking Time:
45 minutes

Serves

12

1 Preheat the oven to 350°F.

2 Steam the vegetables until tender-crisp.

3 Combine ¼ cup of the liquid used for steaming with 1¾ cups milk and pour into a medium saucepan. Mix the cornstarch with the remaining ¼ cup milk and add to the saucepan.

4 Cook over medium heat, stirring constantly, until the mixture boils and thickens. Add the half-and-half. Remove from the heat and stir in the curry powder, sour cream, butter, and salt and pepper to taste.

5 Arrange the vegetables in a shallow 2-quart baking dish and pour the sauce over them. Bake for 45 minutes, until bubbly. Serve hot.

roasted asparagus with lemon zest

WHEN ASPARAGUS COMES INTO THE MARKETS IN THE SPRING, we have this dish at least once a week. The children love to eat the "trees." It is a quick and easy way to get color on the plate, and somehow, asparagus always seems elegant. Look for medium-thick spears for this recipe.

1 tablespoon olive oil
1 pound fresh asparagus,
    trimmed
  Sea salt and freshly ground
    black pepper
1 teaspoon lemon zest

Preparation Time:
5 minutes

Cooking Time:
10 minutes

Serves

1 Preheat the oven to 400°F.

2 Add the olive oil to a shallow roasting pan and roll the asparagus in the oil. Sprinkle with salt and pepper and roast for 10 minutes, shaking once, or until the asparagus is easily pierced and slightly browned.

3 Remove from oven, sprinkle with the zest, and serve.

baked squash casserole

WINTER SQUASH IS ONE OF THE MOST ADAPTABLE and nutritious of foods. Here we add crunch, tang, and sweetness to complement its mild flavor and make a great side dish for roast turkey, chicken, or pork.

4 cups cooked winter squash, such as butternut, hubbard, or pumpkin	1/4 cup nonfat plain yogurt
1 tablespoon butter, softened	1/2 teaspoon salt
3 tablespoons brown sugar	1/4 teaspoon ground nutmeg
	1 egg, slightly beaten
	1/2 cup chopped toasted almonds

1 Preheat oven to 350°F.

2 Mix all the ingredients, except for 2 tablespoons of the almonds, thoroughly but gently in a large bowl. Pour into a 2-quart casserole coated with vegetable cooking spray, top with the reserved almonds, and bake for 30 to 40 minutes, until bubbly. Serve hot.

TIP: To toast the almonds, spread them on the tray of a toaster oven. Set the temperature for 400°F and toast for 5 to 10 minutes, until they are golden brown.

WINTER SQUASH IN THE MICROWAVE
Cut squash into large chunks; remove seeds. Microwave on High in 5-minute bursts until easily pierced with a fork. Scoop out flesh from the skin. Freeze unused portion.

Preparation Time:
15 minutes

Baking Time:
30–40 minutes

Serves

polenta

THE UNKNOWING MIGHT REFER TO POLENTA AS CORNMEAL MUSH. It is a simple Italian dish for which method is everything and cooking is an act of love. Care and patience are essentials for making a good polenta. It is adaptable to many flavors and additions. The best I have ever tasted was at Il Cibreo, a restaurant in Florence, where we had soft polenta as a light lunch. Maybe it was just being in Italy that made it taste so good, but it was simple and divine. Polenta can be served soft right from the pot, or cooled until firm and then fried, or baked with a variety of seasonings and additions. Here is a simple basic soft polenta. Serve it with chicken, fish, or meat, along with vegetables, for a lovely meal.

Cooking Time:
30 minutes

Serves

3 cups skim milk or water

1 teaspoon salt

1 cup stone-ground cornmeal

1 teaspoon butter

¼ cup freshly grated Parmesan cheese or crumbled Gorgonzola

1 Bring the milk to a simmer in a large saucepan over medium-low heat. Add the salt. Very slowly and in a thin stream, add the cornmeal, stirring constantly with a wooden spoon.

2 Lower the heat and cook for about 20 minutes, until the polenta thickens, stirring constantly with a wooden spoon to prevent sticking. The polenta is done when it comes away from the side of the pan as you stir.

3 Add the butter and cheese and stir until they melt. Serve.

hot and cold sesame noodles

ONE MEMORABLE MEAL WITH OLD FRIENDS WAS SALMON, fresh green beans, and these hot and cold sesame noodles. Sitting around a scrubbed wooden table in a farmhouse kitchen, eating this simple meal with folks who hadn't been together in a while, made for a perfect evening. I just don't think the experience would have stayed with me as well if we'd had take-out.

12 ounces spaghetti
1 tablespoon toasted sesame oil
1–2 teaspoons hot chili oil,
    plus more to taste

6 scallions, trimmed, cut on the
    diagonal into 1-inch pieces,
    and sliced in half lengthwise

Prep/Cooking Time:
30 minutes

Serves

SAUCE

1 teaspoon cornstarch
½ cup chicken broth
3 tablespoons rice vinegar

3 tablespoons soy sauce
3 tablespoons Dijon mustard
1 tablespoon dark sesame oil

1   Bring a large pot of salted water to a boil and cook the spaghetti al dente. Drain and toss with the sesame and chili oils in a large bowl; let cool. Toss with the scallions.

2   To make the sauce, cook the cornstarch and chicken broth in a small saucepan over medium heat, stirring until the mixture thickens. Whisk in the remaining ingredients and pour over the pasta. For a spicier dish, add more hot chili oil. Serve at room temperature.

creamy **crunchy** potato bake

THIS RECIPE IS A RESULT OF THE ARRIVAL OF unexpected but demanding guests — guests who like to eat healthy without sacrificing taste. We found that we could create an excellent potato dish without the use of cream and with only a hint of butter.

6 medium potatoes, peeled, boiled until just tender, and cubed (about 4 $\frac{1}{2}$ cups)
2 cups nonfat cottage cheese
1 cup light sour cream or nonfat plain yogurt
1 large garlic clove, minced
2 scallions, finely chopped
2 tablespoons finely chopped fresh chives

Salt and freshly ground white pepper
1 cup lightly buttered breadcrumbs (see Note)
1 cup lightly packed grated cheddar cheese (about 4 ounces)
$\frac{1}{4}$ teaspoon paprika

Preparation Time:
30 minutes

Baking Time:
30 minutes

Serves

1 Preheat the oven to 350°F. Lightly coat the inside of a 9- by 13-inch casserole dish with vegetable cooking spray.

2 Toss the cooked potato cubes with the cottage cheese, sour cream, garlic, scallions, and chives. Add salt and pepper to taste and turn the potato mixture into the prepared casserole dish.

3 Sprinkle with the breadcrumbs and grated cheddar; dust with the paprika. Bake for about 30 minutes, until the top is golden.

NOTE: For the buttered breadcrumbs, melt 2 tablespoons of butter in a skillet over low heat. Remove from the heat and stir in a cup of bread-crumbs until thoroughly coated.

mashed potatoes
á la laura

LAURA, A FRIEND OF KATE'S FROM IDAHO, has been at several of our recent Thanksgiving dinners and taken charge of potato mashing. Our mashed potatoes have never been as smooth and creamy as when Laura makes them. Her tips are: (1) Be sure the potato cooking liquid is evaporated and the potatoes well mashed before adding anything to them; (2) Heat the milk before adding it to the potatoes; and (3) Grow up in Idaho.

8 medium russet potatoes,
   peeled and cut in half
1–3 tablespoons butter
½ cup hot milk
   Salt and freshly ground
   black pepper

Prep/Cooking Time:
30 minutes

Serves

1 Bring a large pot of salted water to a boil and cook the potatoes for about 20 minutes, or until they are tender when pierced with a fork. Drain the potatoes and return them to the pot.

2 Over very low heat, mash the potatoes with a potato masher until they seem quite dry. Add the butter and hot milk; mash and beat with the potato masher until they are smooth and creamy. Serve immediately.

overnight baked
mashed potatoes

ANA PUT ME ON TO THIS WHEN WE WERE CATERING A DINNER FOR 120 PEOPLE. She said that if you put enough butter/sour cream/cheese in the cooked potatoes, they will freeze beautifully and reheat perfectly. Russets are the best because they are dry and fluffy when cooked.

Preparation Time:
40 minutes

Sitting Time:
1 hour

Baking Time:
35 minutes

Serves

3 ⅓ pounds russet potatoes (about 4 large), washed, peeled, and cut into quarters
½ cup whole milk, heated
2 tablespoons butter, plus more for the dish

½ cup sour cream or 4 ounces goat cheese
½ teaspoon salt
Freshly ground black pepper

1 Bring a large pot of salted water to a boil. Add the potatoes and cook until they are easily pierced with a fork, 20 to 30 minutes. Drain the potatoes and return them to the pot.

2 Over very low heat, mash the potatoes with a potato masher until thoroughly soft and smooth, to dry them out but not brown them. Add the warm milk to the pot and continue mashing. Add the butter, sour cream, salt, and pepper, and keep mashing until completely blended.

3 Transfer the potatoes to a buttered 2-quart casserole dish. Cover with aluminum foil and refrigerate for up to 1 day, or freeze for up to 1 month.

4 When ready to cook, thaw if necessary and let sit at room temperature for 1 hour before baking. Stir if it looks watery.

5 Preheat the oven to 350°F. Bake the potatoes, covered, for 20 minutes, then uncover and bake for 15 minutes longer, or until thoroughly hot.

skinny french fries
or sweet potato fries

THESE ARE A GREAT ALTERNATIVE TO GREASY FRENCH FRIES and a big hit with fast-food lovers! They are here especially for the young folks, but I guarantee that all ages will love them. For a tasty alternative, use sweet potatoes (see below).

6 medium Idaho potatoes
2 teaspoons canola oil
   Salt and freshly ground
   black pepper

Preparation Time:
20 minutes

Cooking Time:
20 minutes

Serves

1 Preheat the oven to 400°F. Coat a large baking sheet or sheets with vegetable cooking spray.

2 Peel the potatoes and cut lengthwise into ¼-inch sticks. Toss the potatoes with the oil in a large bowl, making sure all the pieces are coated with oil.

3 Spread the potatoes on the baking sheet and bake for 20 minutes, or until they are soft on the inside and slightly browned on the outside. Season with salt and pepper to taste and serve immediately.

✕ SWEET POTATO FRIES

Follow the directions for French fries, but toss the sweet potatoes with a spice mix of ½ teaspoon ground cumin, ¼ teaspoon chili powder, and a pinch of ground cayenne pepper, for a spicy result that goes beautifully with grilled chicken or fish.

potato **gratin**

MY MOTHER-IN-LAW USED TO MAKE WONDERFUL SCALLOPED POTATOES, which is a creamy layered dish with a crunchy top. Many think that a gratin implies a cheesy topping, but it is really just a French version of scalloped potatoes. Gratins are not limited to potatoes either; any vegetable can be sliced, layered, combined with a béchamel sauce and maybe some breadcrumbs, and baked. In this case the sauce forms as the ingredients come together during baking. Since it is rich and creamy, serve it with a simple chicken, meat, or fish dish.

8 cups thinly sliced unpeeled red
potatoes (about 6 large)
$\frac{1}{4}$ cup all-purpose flour
$\frac{1}{2}$ cup finely chopped fresh parsley
1 large onion, thinly sliced

$\frac{1}{2}$ teaspoon salt
Freshly ground black pepper
1 teaspoon butter
2 cups low-fat milk

Preparation Time:
30 minutes

Baking Time:
1 hour

Serves

1   Preheat the oven to 350°F. Lightly coat a shallow 2-quart baking dish with vegetable cooking spray.

2   Pat the potatoes dry with paper towels. Toss them in a large bowl with the flour, parsley, and onion slices until the potatoes and onions are coated with flour and the herbs are distributed throughout.

3   Arrange the potatoes in overlapping layers in the baking dish. Season with the salt and pepper and dot with the butter. Pour the milk over the potatoes until it just covers them but does not rise above them. Cover the pan with aluminum foil and bake for 1 hour, or until the potatoes are tender.

baked potatoes with assorted toppings

HERE THE LOWLY SPUD IS TAKEN TO NEW HEIGHTS, with surprises inside and decorations outside. For people who can't decide how they want their potato, they can have it all with this recipe.

8 large baking potatoes
$1/2$–$3/4$ cup crumbled herbed goat cheese (5-ounce log)
Olive oil

Coarse salt
Toppings of your choice

Preparation Time:
15 minutes

Baking Time:
1 hour

Serves

1 Preheat the oven to 400°F.

2 With an apple corer, remove a plug from the center of half of the potatoes, boring in from both ends. Save the pieces. Pack a tablespoon of goat cheese into each cavity and plug each end with a reserved potato piece, trimming the pieces to fit.

3 Brush the potatoes with olive oil and sprinkle with a small amount of salt. Bake for 1 hour, or until tender when pierced with a fork.

4 Serve hot with assorted toppings.

TOPPINGS

- Salsa (see pages 30 and 33)
- Mixture of half nonfat plain yogurt and half light sour cream
- Chopped steamed broccoli
- Freshly grated Parmesan cheese
- Chopped fresh herbs of your choice: chives, dill, basil, cilantro
- Low-fat cottage cheese or ricotta cheese

broiled potatoes

THIS IS A QUICK AND EASY potato gratin.

10 medium red potatoes
½–¾ cup grated Gruyére cheese
(2–3 ounces)
Salt and freshly ground
black pepper

Prep/Cooking Time:
30 minutes

Serves

1 Bring a large pot of salted water to a boil. Boil the potatoes until fork-tender,
15 to 20 minutes. Drain and allow to cool until you can handle them.

2 Preheat the broiler. Lightly coat a shallow 10-inch pie pan with vegetable
cooking spray.

3 Slice the potatoes and arrange in the pie pan. Scatter the cheese, salt,
and pepper over the top and place the pan 6 inches from the broiler for
5 minutes, or until the cheese melts. Serve hot.

THANKSGIVING MENU

- Turkey with Cranberry, Apple,
  Sage, and Onion Stuffing
  (page 191)
- Mashed Potatoes á la Laura
  (page 185)
- Curried Brussels Sprouts and
  Cauliflower (page 179)
- Baked Squash Casserole
  (page 181)

- Creamed onions
- Golden Harvest Vegetables
  (page 178)
- Baby peas
- Cranberry Salsa (page 155)
- Crunch-Top Apple Pie (page 194)
- Pumpkin pie

cranberry, **apple**, sage, and **onion stuffing**

I AM A GREAT BELIEVER IN MAKING THINGS FROM SCRATCH — with a few exceptions. One of these exceptions is stuffing. Pepperidge Farm Herbed Stuffing Mix is delicious as is or with some embellishment. I always doctor it up, and these are some of my favorite additions for a roast turkey stuffing.

8 cups herbed stuffing mix
2 celery stalks, chopped
1 large onion, chopped
4 apples, peeled, cored, and chopped
1½ teaspoons dried rubbed sage
1 teaspoon dried thyme
½ teaspoon salt
¼ teaspoon freshly ground black pepper
1 cup chopped cranberries
2 tablespoons butter
1½ cups water

Preparation Time:
15 minutes

Baking Time:
1 hour

Makes

cups
(enough to stuff a 12-pound turkey)

1 If you are cooking the stuffing separately, preheat the oven to 350°F.

2 Place the stuffing mix in a very large bowl. Add the celery, onion, apples, sage, thyme, salt, pepper, and cranberries. Mix well with a large wooden spoon or your hands.

3 Heat the butter in the water in a cup in the microwave, and pour over the stuffing mix; stir lightly with a fork.

4 If you are cooking the stuffing separately, put it into a 3-quart baking dish and bake for 1 hour. If you are cooking the stuffing in a turkey, loosely pack the cavity of the turkey just before putting the turkey into the oven. Cook the turkey according to its package directions, or use your favorite method. Put any extra stuffing in a casserole dish and bake with the turkey for the last hour.

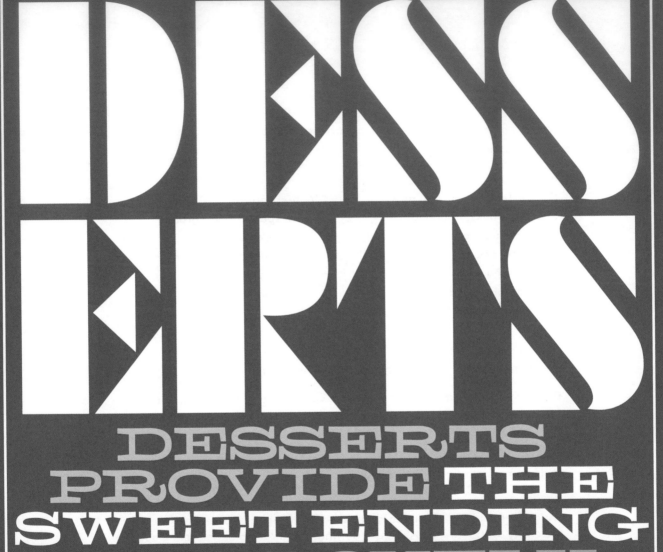

DESSERTS

DESSERTS PROVIDE THE SWEET ENDING TO A LOVELY MEAL.

They can be as simple as a luscious piece of ripe fruit in season, a savory wedge of cheese, or a favorite ice cream. Or, when going "over the top," it can be a big flashy dessert. Our flashy desserts make a sensational presentation, and they take some time, but they can be made ahead. And they rank very high on the delectable scale. Anytime desserts are no less delicious and satisfying to the sweet tooth, but are simpler to make.

In the never-ending search for the "perfect" chocolate chip cookie, there are four to choose from here, as well as cobblers and cakes, fruit-centric desserts, and more.

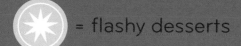 = flashy desserts

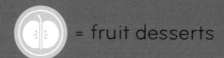 = fruit desserts

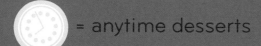 = anytime desserts

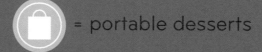 = portable desserts

crunch-top apple pie

SOMETIMES WE GET TIRED OF TRADITIONAL APPLE PIE, wonderful though it is. For those who love walnuts and apples, this is the pie for you. Plus, there is only one piecrust to make (or buy). And besides all that, this is a most tasty pie — especially if you select juicy, tart baking apples.

6 tart baking apples, peeled, cored, and sliced
1 cup nonfat plain yogurt
1 egg, beaten

½ cup granulated sugar
¼ cup all-purpose flour
1 unbaked 9-inch piecrust

Preparation Time:
30 minutes

Baking Time:
50–60 minutes

Makes

1

9-inch
pie

TOPPING

4 tablespoons (½ stick) unsalted butter, melted
⅓ cup granulated sugar
⅓ cup light or dark brown sugar

½ cup all-purpose flour
1 teaspoon ground cinnamon
½ cup chopped walnuts

1 Preheat the oven to 450°F.

2 Toss the apples with the yogurt, egg, sugar, and flour in a large bowl until well coated.

3 Pour the apple mixture into the piecrust and bake for 10 minutes. Turn the oven down to 350°F and bake for 35 to 40 minutes.

4 Mix the topping ingredients together in a medium bowl and sprinkle over the pie. Bake for an additional 15 to 20 minutes, until the topping is lightly browned. Cool the pie on a wire rack.

sarah's **peanut butter** pie

PEANUT BUTTER FOR DESSERT? A wonderful contrast of flavors and textures, this is one of those recipes we treasure, where the creating is fast and fun and the results are memorable.

1/3 cup creamy peanut butter
1/2 cup light corn syrup
1 quart vanilla frozen yogurt or
   light ice cream, softened

2/3 cup unsalted dry-roasted
   peanuts
1 (9-inch) graham cracker crust,
   baked (page 200)

1 Blend the peanut butter and corn syrup together in a small bowl.

2 Alternate layers of frozen yogurt, peanut butter, and peanuts in the pie crust, beginning with half the softened yogurt, half the peanut butter, and half the peanuts.

3 Cover tightly with plastic wrap and freeze for at least 5 hours before serving.

Preparation Time:
20 minutes

Freezing Time:
5 hours

Makes
1
9-inch
pie

MENU FOR A COOKOUT AT THE BEACH

- Grilled turkey sausages
- Lemon Chicken and Vegetable Kabobs (page 128)
- Basmati rice
- Sliced Garden Tomatoes with Herbed Caper Vinaigrette (page 60)
- Sarah's Peanut Butter Pie

mountainous birthday cake with boiled icing

THIS VERY TALL, SPECTACULAR-LOOKING BIRTHDAY CAKE was a tradition when I was growing up. By the second day, if there is any left, the icing develops a crunchy outer layer that shatters when cut. As one who usually loves a variety of textures, colors, and flavors, I can't explain my love of this sweet all-white cake, but it's delicious and worthy of a special event! Decorate it with fresh edible flowers or a bunch of tall, slender, brightly colored taper candles.

Preparation Time:
30 minutes

Baking Time:
30–35 minutes

Makes

1

9-inch double
layer cake

CAKE

$^1/_2$ cup vegetable shortening

$1^1/_2$ cups sugar

4 egg yolks, well beaten (reserve the whites for the icing)

1 teaspoon vanilla extract

3 cups sifted cake flour

4 teaspoons baking powder

$^1/_2$ teaspoon salt

$1^1/_4$ cups skim milk

ICING

2 cups granulated sugar

$^3/_4$ cup water

1 tablespoon light corn syrup

5 egg whites (or pasteurized egg whites; see Note)

2 tablespoons confectioners' sugar

1 teaspoon vanilla extract

1 Preheat the oven to 375°F. Coat two 9-inch round cake pans with vegetable cooking spray.

2 Beat the shortening and sugar together in a large bowl until light and fluffy. Add the egg yolks and vanilla; continue beating until well mixed.

3 Sift the flour, baking powder, and salt together in a medium bowl. Add the flour to the egg mixture, alternating with the milk, and stirring between each addition. Stir until the batter is smooth.

4 Pour the batter into the two pans and bake for 30 to 35 minutes, or until the cake is lightly golden and separated from the edge of the pan, and springs back in the center when lightly touched.

5 To make the icing, boil the granulated sugar, water, and corn syrup in a large uncovered saucepan, without stirring, over medium heat. Cook until the syrup spins a thread (see Note). Remove from heat.

6 While the syrup is cooking, beat the egg whites with an electric mixer until stiff peaks form; beat in the confectioners' sugar.

7 Slowly pour the boiling syrup over the egg whites, beating constantly. Add the vanilla. When the beaters leave tracks in the icing, it is stiff enough to spread.

8 Cool the layers for 10 minutes in the pans on cooling racks. Remove from the pans and cool completely on racks. Place one layer of cake upside down on a large plate. Cover with about one-third of the icing (it will be $1/2$ to 1 inch thick). Center the other cake on the iced layer; spread the top with a thick layer of icing and then ice the sides.

NOTE ON EGGS: If you are concerned about using uncooked eggs, use the 7-minute method. Place all the icing ingredients except for the vanilla in the top of a double boiler over 1 inch of simmering water on medium heat. Beat constantly with an electric mixer for about 7 minutes, until the beaters leave a track. Mix in the vanilla.

NOTE ON SUGAR SYRUP THREADS: Stir the syrup with a wooden spoon; hold the spoon over the pan. If a coarse thread hangs down from the spoon, the syrup is at the crucial, thread-spinning stage. Be careful not to burn the syrup.

drop dead brownies

AFTER MAKING MANY BATCHES OF BROWNIES using standard unsweetened baking chocolate, very expensive high-quality baking chocolate, more sugar, less sugar, more butter, less butter, and oil, and then sifting through the opinions of tasters, we have determined that the brownie we all like best is my old brownie recipe with regular baking chocolate and lots of sugar and butter. The expensive chocolate had a more lasting chocolate flavor, but no one felt it justified the significant cost increase. The method is very simple and produces a moist, chewy, and very chocolatey brownie.

4 ounces unsweetened
    baking chocolate
1 cup (2 sticks) unsalted butter
2 cups sugar
2 teaspoons vanilla extract

1 teaspoon salt
4 eggs
1 cup all-purpose flour
3/4 cup chopped walnuts
    (optional)

Preparation Time:
15 minutes

Baking Time:
30 minutes

Makes
24
medium

or

48
mini brownies

1   Preheat the oven to 350°F. Spray a 9- by 13-inch baking pan with vegetable cooking spray.

2   Place the chocolate and butter in a large saucepan over low heat. Stir occasionally with a wooden spoon as the chocolate and butter melt. Remove from the heat when melted and stir in the sugar, vanilla, and salt. Stir until completely blended. Add the eggs one a time, mixing in completely before adding the next one. Stir in the flour completely, and add the nuts, if desired.

3   Scrape the batter into the prepared pan and bake for 25 to 30 minutes, until the edges pull away from the sides of the pan and a skewer inserted in the center comes out almost clean. Do not overbake, or the brownies will dry out. Remove from the oven, cool on a rack, and cut into squares.

cheater's chocolate cake

THIS RETRO RECIPE DEPENDS ON PREPARED MIXES, but the resulting moist and rich chocolate Bundt cake gives no hint of its mundane origins. Yes, we do admit to "cheating" and taking the easy road, but this is such a great recipe for kids (of all ages) that we just had to include it. This is not only a great dessert but also a wonderful bake sale contribution or a warm welcome for new neighbors.

1 teaspoon unsweetened
  cocoa powder
1 (18.25-ounce) package devil's
  food cake mix
1 (3.4-ounce) package instant
  chocolate pudding mix
1 cup sour cream

1/2 cup vegetable oil
1/2 cup water
4 eggs, beaten
1 cup semisweet chocolate chips
  Confectioners' sugar for
  dusting (optional)

1 Preheat the oven to 350°F. Spray a 12-cup Bundt pan with vegetable cooking spray and dust with the cocoa powder.

2 Combine all of the remaining ingredients except for the chocolate chips and confectioners' sugar in a large bowl. Beat for 4 minutes. Fold in the chips.

3 Pour the batter into the prepared pan and bake for 50 to 60 minutes, until an inserted toothpick comes out clean. Cool in the pan for 15 minutes and then turn out onto a serving plate. Dust with confectioners' sugar, if desired.

Preparation Time:
15 minutes

Baking Time:
50–60 minutes

Makes

1

Bundt
cake

lemon chiffon pie

NOBODY BELIEVES THAT THIS WONDERFULLY LIGHT DESSERT isn't dripping with calories. Yes, you could use heavy cream instead of evaporated skim milk to get a richer mouth-feel, but the light, bright freshness of this pie stands on its own. Now that I live in California and have a lemon tree, it's an even bigger favorite.

GRAHAM CRACKER CRUST

20 graham crackers, crushed into fine crumbs (about 1⅓ cups; roll in a plastic bag or process in a food processor)

2 tablespoons sugar

1 tablespoon water

1 tablespoon egg white, slightly beaten

2 tablespoons canola oil

Preparation Time:
30 minutes

Freezing Time:
8 hours

Makes

1

9-inch
pie

FILLING

¾ cup sugar

¼ cup corn syrup

2 tablespoons water

½ cup very cold evaporated skim milk

3 egg whites or pasteurized egg whites, at room temperature

¾ cup cold orange juice

2 teaspoons lemon zest

Juice of 2 lemons (about ½ cup), chilled

1   Preheat the oven to 350°F.

2   To make the crust, combine all the crust ingredients in a medium bowl; mix with your fingers until the crumbs are uniformly moistened. Press the crumbs into the bottom and up the sides of a 9-inch pie pan. Bake for 8 to 10 minutes, or until lightly browned. Cool on a wire rack.

3 To make the filling, mix the sugar, corn syrup, and water in a small saucepan; cook over medium heat until simmering. Cover and boil for about 1 minute. Uncover and continue simmering, without stirring, until the syrup reaches the a soft-ball stage, 240°F on a candy thermometer, 1 to 2 minutes. Remove from the heat and set aside.

4 In a small chilled bowl and with chilled beaters, beat the cold milk until it forms soft peaks. Set aside.

5 Thoroughly clean and dry the beaters. Beat the egg whites in a medium bowl until soft peaks form. Reheat the syrup until just boiling. Continue beating the egg whites on high speed while carefully pouring in the hot syrup in a steady stream. Keep beating until mixture becomes thick, fluffy, and smooth, and forms stiff peaks.

6 Fold in the orange juice, lemon zest, lemon juice, and whipped milk. Pile the filling into the graham cracker crust and freeze for 8 hours or overnight. Let the pie sit out for a little while to soften before slicing and serving.

chocolate **angel cake** with **toppings**

DUTCHING IS A PROCESS THAT NEUTRALIZES THE ACIDITY in cocoa powder and produces a powder both darker and mellower than traditional cocoa powder. You'll find that using it in this recipe results in a cake light enough to avoid guilt, yet rich enough to delight your chocolate lovers.

$^3/_4$ cup cake flour
$^1/_4$ cup Dutch-processed
    cocoa powder
$1^1/_4$ cups sugar
10 egg whites, at room temperature

$^1/_4$ teaspoon salt
1 teaspoon cream of tartar
$^1/_2$ teaspoon vanilla extract

Preparation Time:
30 minutes

Baking Time:
35 minutes

Makes

1

10-inch
pie

1   Place a baking rack in the center of the oven. Preheat the oven to 350°F.

2   Sift together the flour and cocoa powder until well blended. Add $^1/_4$ cup of the sugar and sift again into a large bowl; set aside.

3   Gently beat the egg whites with the salt in a clean bowl. Add the cream of tartar and increase the beater speed. Beat until soft peaks form when the beaters are raised. Gradually beat in the remaining 1 cup sugar, a tablespoon at a time, until stiff peaks form. Blend in the vanilla.

4   Sift a little of the flour mixture over the egg whites and fold it in with a large spatula. Repeat this process until all the flour is incorporated. Do

not fold the mixture more than necessary, as too much mixing will keep the cake from rising.

5 Gently transfer the batter to an ungreased 10-inch tube pan. Bake for 35 minutes without opening the oven door. Test with a toothpick after 35 minutes; it should come out clean, and cake center should spring back when lightly pressed.

6 When done, invert the cake and suspend the pan by placing the opening in the center of the tube pan over the neck of an empty wine bottle. Allow to cool for at least $1\frac{1}{2}$ hours. Loosen the cake from the sides of the pan very carefully with a sharp knife and remove from pan. To serve, gently pull the cake apart with two forks or slice carefully with a serrated knife. Top with Raspberry Purée, Cocoa Cream, or both (recipes follow on page 204).

MENU FOR A NEW YEAR'S EVE BUFFET ✕

- **Strawberry Party Punch** (page 245)
- **Iced tea, fresh lemonade, sparkling water, and Champagne**
- **Sliced Smoked Salmon with Yogurt Spread (page 34)**
- **Capers, sliced onions, and rye crackers**

- **Sliced Beef Tenderloin (page 138)**
- **Shrimp and Feta Casserole (page 115)**
- **Spinach Salad with Poppy Seed Dressing (page 74)**
- **Bread basket**
- **Chocolate Angel Cake with Toppings**

RASPBERRY PURÉE

Preparation Time: 10 minutes • Makes 2 cups

- 1 (10-ounce) package frozen unsweetened raspberries
- 1 teaspoon kirsch

Purée the raspberries in a blender or food processor. If you prefer seedless, press the mixture through a sieve. Stir in the kirsch. Chill until ready to serve.

COCOA CREAM

Preparation Time: 15 minutes • Serves 8

- 1 cup heavy cream
- ¼ cup confectioners' sugar, sifted
- ¼ cup unsweetened cocoa powder
- ½ cup low-fat plain yogurt

Chill the mixing bowl and beaters in freezer.

Mix together the cream, sugar, and cocoa powder in the chilled bowl. Beat with the chilled beaters until stiff enough to hold a peak; blend in the yogurt and chill thoroughly. Pile in a pretty glass serving bowl and allow guests to top their angel cake with a dollop.

NOTE: To cut out the fat, try beating 1½ cups ice-cold evaporated skim milk in place of the cream and then adding all the other ingredients except the yogurt.

white chocolate cranberry oatmeal cookies

ON MY QUEST for the perfect cookie, this is at the top of the list.

³/₄ cup (1¹/₂ sticks) unsalted
   butter, softened
¹/₂ cup brown sugar
¹/₂ cup granulated sugar
 1 egg
 2 tablespoons water
 1 teaspoon vanilla extract
1³/₄ cups unbleached all-purpose
   flour
 1 teaspoon baking soda

¹/₂ teaspoon baking powder
¹/₂ teaspoon salt
³/₄ cups dried cranberries
³/₄ cup rolled oats
³/₄ cup chopped pecans
¹/₂ cup sweetened flaked coconut
 6 ounces white chocolate cut into
   small chunks, or 1 cup white
   chocolate chips

1 Preheat the oven to 325°F. Line baking sheets with parchment paper.

2 Beat the butter and sugars in a large bowl for several minutes until they are light and fluffy. Add the egg, water, and vanilla, and beat for another minute. Place a wire strainer over the bowl and combine the flour, baking soda, baking powder, and salt in the strainer. Sift into the butter mixture, and beat on low speed until well mixed.

3 Stir in the cranberries, oats, pecans, coconut, and chocolate.

4 Shape the dough into walnut-size balls. Place on the prepared pans and flatten into disks with wet fingers. Bake for 10 to 12 minutes, or until the edges are golden and the tops look dry, but the cookies are still soft inside. Cool the pan on a rack for 1 minute before transferring the cookies from the pan to the cooling rack.

Preparation Time:
20 minutes

Baking Time:
12 minutes

Makes
36
cookies

apple sports cake

I ONCE OFFERED THIS MOIST, FLAVORFUL CAKE under another name to Kate's friends Chris, a runner, and Laura and Carrie. Chris declined, but when Carrie called it "sports cake," he gobbled up three pieces. It's had that name ever since!

1 egg	¹/₂ teaspoon salt
2 egg whites	2 teaspoons baking soda
1 cup granulated sugar	1 teaspoon ground cinnamon
¹/₂ cup canola oil	1 teaspoon ground allspice
¹/₂ cup apple butter	3 cups grated apples (peeled
2 cups all-purpose flour	or unpeeled)
²/₃ cup whole wheat pastry flour	1 cup raisins
3 tablespoons unsweetened	¹/₂ cup chopped pecans
cocoa powder	Confectioners' sugar

Preparation Time:
30 minutes

Baking Time:
1 hour

Makes

1

10-inch
Bundt
cake

1 Preheat the oven to 350°F. Coat a 10-inch Bundt pan with vegetable cooking spray and dust with flour.

2 Whisk together the egg, egg whites, sugar, oil, and apple butter in a large bowl. Sift the flours, cocoa powder, salt, baking soda, cinnamon, and allspice together in a smaller bowl.

3 Add the dry ingredients and apples to the egg mixture by alternating additions between the dry ingredients and the apples, stirring well after each addition. The batter will be very thick. Stir in the raisins and nuts. Spoon the batter into the prepared pan.

4 Bake for 1 hour, or until a skewer inserted in the center comes out clean. Cool the cake on a wire rack for 10 minutes, and then remove from the pan and allow to cool completely. Dust with confectioners' sugar before serving.

lemonade pie

THE FRONT PORCH OF OUR BEACH HOUSE has been the site of many, many lemonade stands. Here is another truly delectable use for frozen lemonade. The tart lemon and creamy vanilla combined with a hint of apricots make an easy-to-prepare fresh and delightful end to a summer barbecue.

1 (10-ounce) jar apricot preserves
1 (6-ounce) can frozen lemonade
  concentrate, thawed
½ gallon vanilla frozen yogurt,
  slightly softened

2 fully baked 9-inch pie shells
  Chocolate curls for garnish
  (optional)

1 Heat the apricot preserves in the microwave until they just become liquid. Let cool slightly.

2 Quickly blend the preserves, lemonade concentrate, and frozen yogurt together, keeping the yogurt from thawing any more than is necessary.

3 Fill the pie shells with the yogurt mixture; cover tightly with plastic wrap and freeze until ready to serve. Sprinkle the pies with chocolate curls before serving, if desired.

Preparation Time:
15 minutes

Freezing Time:
2 hours

Makes

9-inch
pies

mom's favorite **gingerbread** with **hot lemon** sauce

JOHN'S MOM BAKED A LOT AND LOVED TO FEED the delicacies to her two growing sons. This lovely, high-rising, fragrant gingerbread is one of their favorites. The hot lemon sauce is a wonderful counterpoint to the spicy cake, and I can't believe that I like it better than whipped cream on gingerbread.

2 eggs
³/₄ cup brown sugar
³/₄ cup molasses
¹/₂ cup canola oil
1 teaspoon grated fresh gingerroot
2 ¹/₃ cups unbleached all-purpose
    flour
2 teaspoons ground ginger

1 teaspoon ground cinnamon
¹/₄ teaspoon ground nutmeg
¹/₈ teaspoon ground cloves
2 teaspoons baking soda
¹/₂ teaspoon baking powder
¹/₂ teaspoon salt
1 cup boiling water

Preparation Time:
10 minutes

Baking Time:
40 minutes

Makes

16
large squares

LEMON SAUCE
1 cup water
¹/₂ cup granulated sugar
1 tablespoon cornstarch

2 tablespoons unsalted butter
2 tablespoons lemon juice
1 teaspoon lemon zest

1 Preheat the oven to 350°F. Coat a 9- by 9-inch baking pan with vegetable cooking spray.

2 Beat together the eggs, sugar, molasses, oil, and fresh ginger in a large bowl. Combine the flour, ground ginger, cinnamon, nutmeg, cloves,

baking soda, baking powder, and salt in a strainer, and sift into the egg mixture. Using an electric mixer, blend thoroughly. Add the boiling water and beat for another 20 seconds. Pour the batter into the prepared pan and bake for 35 to 40 minutes, or until the cake pulls away from the sides of the pan and a skewer inserted in the center comes out clean. Don't overbake. Let cool in the pan on a wire rack.

3   While the cake is baking, make the sauce by stirring the water, sugar, and cornstarch together in a small saucepan over medium-high heat. Cook for about 4 minutes, or until the mixture boils and becomes clear. Remove from the heat and add the butter, lemon juice, and zest. Stir and serve over the warm gingerbread.

WARMING MEAL FOR A FRIEND IN NEED ✕

- Cream of Chicken Soup (page 82)
- Big Green Salad with Jeanne's Dressing (pages 74 and 75)
- Mom's Gingerbread with Hot Lemon Sauce

featherweight cupcakes

THIS IS ONE OF THE FEW RECIPES I have found where children will eat both cake *and* frosting.

1 cup cake flour
1/2 cup sugar
1 1/2 teaspoons baking soda
1/4 teaspoon salt
2 egg yolks

1 tablespoon orange zest
1/3 cup orange juice
2 tablespoons vegetable oil
4 egg whites
1/4 teaspoon cream of tartar

FROSTING

6 ounces light cream cheese
1 tablespoon orange juice

1 tablespoon honey

Preparation Time:
30 minutes

Baking Time:
16–18 minutes

Makes
12
cupcakes

1   Preheat the oven to 325°F. Line 12 muffin wells with baking cups.

2   Sift the flour, sugar, baking soda, and salt together in a medium bowl. Make a well in the center. Whisk together the egg yolks, orange zest, orange juice, and vegetable oil in a small bowl; pour into the well. Beat until thoroughly blended.

3   In a separate bowl, with clean beaters, whip the egg whites and cream of tartar until they are very stiff. Gently fold the egg whites into the batter, 1 cupful at a time. Mix only until the whites and batter are incorporated; excessive mixing may cause the whites to collapse.

4   Spoon the batter into the muffin wells up to the top; bake immediately. Check the cupcakes after about 15 minutes; they are done when a toothpick inserted in the center comes out clean. Cool on wire racks.

5   To make the frosting, mix together the cream cheese, orange juice, and honey in a small bowl, and spread on the cupcake tops. Top with raisins, chopped fruit, jelly beans, or chopped nuts, if desired.

mocha pudding cake

THIS UNIQUE CAKE IS ANOTHER RECIPE from John's mom. The miracle of pudding cake is that a lovely sauce forms at the bottom of the cake, which can be spooned over the top when served. It is simple to make, and it's best served warm.

2 eggs

$\frac{1}{2}$ cup milk

3 tablespoons unsalted butter, melted

1 teaspoon vanilla extract

1 cup unbleached all-purpose flour

$\frac{1}{2}$ cup granulated sugar

2 teaspoons baking powder

1 teaspoon ground cinnamon

$\frac{1}{2}$ teaspoon ground allspice

$\frac{1}{4}$ teaspoon ground nutmeg

$\frac{1}{8}$ teaspoon ground cloves

$\frac{1}{4}$ teaspoon salt

TOPPING

$\frac{1}{3}$ cup light or dark brown sugar

$\frac{1}{3}$ cup granulated sugar

$\frac{1}{4}$ cup cocoa powder

1 cup cold brewed coffee

Preparation Time:
10 minutes

Baking Time:
30 minutes

Makes
1
8-inch-square
cake

1 Preheat the oven to 350°F. Coat an 8- by 8-inch baking pan with vegetable cooking spray.

2 Whisk together the eggs, milk, butter, and vanilla in a large bowl. Put the flour, sugar, baking powder, cinnamon, allspice, nutmeg, cloves, and salt in a wire strainer and sift into the egg mixture. Stir batter until thoroughly blended. Pour the batter into the prepared pan.

3 To make the topping, mix the sugars and cocoa powder together in a small bowl and scatter over the batter. Pour the coffee over all. Bake for 30 minutes, or until a skewer inserted in the center comes out clean. Cool slightly on a rack. Spoon the warm cake onto dessert plates.

NOTE: If made ahead, the cake can be warmed in a 200°F oven for 5 minutes before serving.

flourless chocolate raspberry torte

THIS DELICIOUS CAKE IS UNASHAMEDLY RICH. Some recipes are better left untampered with, and this is one of them. Serve small slices and enjoy every crumb. It has been my daughter Kate's favorite birthday cake since she was old enough to appreciate chocolate. This torte has two layers, and it uses ground walnuts instead of flour.

6 eggs, separated
3/4 cup granulated sugar
1 3/4 cups ground walnuts

1/4 cup semisweet chocolate pieces
3 tablespoons strong hot coffee

FROSTING

4 tablespoons (1/2 stick) unsalted butter, softened
3/4 cup sifted confectioners' sugar
1/4 cup semisweet chocolate pieces

3 tablespoons strong hot coffee
1 teaspoon vanilla extract
2 tablespoons seedless raspberry jam

Preparation Time:
30 minutes

Baking Time:
1 hour

Makes
1
10-inch
cake

1   Preheat the oven to 350°F. Coat the bottom and sides of a 10-inch round cake pan with a removable bottom with vegetable cooking spray. Dust with flour.

2   Beat the egg whites in a medium bowl until soft peaks form. In a large bowl, beat 5 of the egg yolks with the sugar until thick, lemon-colored, and light. (Reserve the extra yolk for another use.) Add half of the ground walnuts.

3 Melt the chocolate bits in the hot coffee and add slowly to the egg yolk mixture. Stir in a few tablespoons of the egg whites and mix well. Gently fold in the remaining egg whites and the remaining walnuts.

4 Spoon the cake batter into the prepared pan and bake for 1 hour, or until a cake tester comes out clean. Remove from the pan and cool on a wire rack.

5 While the cake is cooling, make the frosting. Beat the butter and sugar together in a medium bowl until smooth and fluffy. Melt the chocolate bits in the hot coffee and add to the butter mixture. Add the vanilla. Mix well.

6 When the cake is completely cool, slice it horizontally into two layers with a long serrated knife. Place the bottom layer on a pretty cake plate. Spread with the raspberry jam, then top with a thin layer of frosting. Set the other layer on top and frost completely with the remaining frosting. Store in the refrigerator.

MENU FOR A SHOWER OR ENGAGEMENT PARTY

- Wedding Cake Cheese (page 34)
- Crudités with Salsa Verde (page 30)
- Grilled Salmon with Mustard Sauce (page 157)
- Northern Italian Lasagna (page 116)
- Green and Orange Salad (page 57)
- Crusty whole wheat rolls
- Flourless Chocolate Raspberry Torte
- Sparkling juices
- Champagne

cranapple **walnut** cake

MMM, YOUR KITCHEN WILL SMELL SO GOOD! This rich and moist cake is a delicious step away from its popular cousin, the carrot cake. Any variety of apples will work, but I like Golden Delicious and McIntosh and have used them both separately and combined. This cake is a good traveler. While it is delicious served warm with a scoop of vanilla frozen yogurt or ice cream, I like it best plain.

$\frac{1}{2}$ cup light brown sugar

$\frac{1}{2}$ cup granulated sugar

1 egg

$\frac{1}{3}$ cup canola oil

1 cup whole wheat pastry flour
    or all-purpose flour

$\frac{1}{2}$ teaspoon salt

1 teaspoon baking soda

1 teaspoon ground cinnamon

$\frac{1}{4}$ teaspoon ground nutmeg

$\frac{1}{2}$ cup coarsely chopped cranberries

2 cups shredded unpeeled apples
    (about 5 medium)

1 cup chopped walnuts

Preparation Time:
30 minutes

Baking Time:
45 minutes

Makes

1

8-inch
square
cake

1 Preheat the oven to 350°F. Coat an 8- by 8-inch pan with vegetable cooking spray.

2 Cream the sugars and egg together by hand in a large bowl; blend in the oil. Combine the flour, salt, baking soda, cinnamon, and nutmeg in another bowl and add to the sugar-egg mixture. Mix by hand. The mixture will be quite stiff. Toss together the cranberries, shredded apples, and walnuts in a bowl and fold into the batter.

3 Turn the batter into the prepared pan and bake for 45 minutes. Cool on a wire rack for 10 minutes; serve warm.

awesome blueberry pie

MANY BLUEBERRIES GRACE THIS WONDERFULLY FRESH-TASTING and quickly assembled pie. If you live where you can get wild blueberries, you are indeed lucky, and I highly recommend using them; their flavor is superb. However, fresh cultivated berries will also be wonderful. Serve it on lovely dessert plates with perfectly round balls of French vanilla ice cream.

2 quarts blueberries
$\frac{1}{2}$ cup granulated sugar
$\frac{1}{2}$ cup brown sugar
$\frac{1}{4}$ teaspoon ground cinnamon
$\frac{1}{4}$ teaspoon salt
1 teaspoon unsalted butter
2 tablespoons cornstarch

2 tablespoons lemon juice
1 fully baked 10-inch pie shell
   (use pie dough found in the
   refrigerated section of the
   supermarket, or make your
   favorite recipe)

1 Mix together 1 quart of the blueberries, the sugars, cinnamon, salt, and butter in a large saucepan and mash slightly. Dissolve the cornstarch in the lemon juice and add to the mixture. Cook over medium heat until the mixture bubbles and thickens. Cook for 5 minutes longer, stirring frequently.

2 Cool the blueberry mixture and then add the remaining uncooked blueberries. Fill the pie shell and chill before serving.

Prep/Cooking Time:
20 minutes

Makes
1
10-inch
pie

luscious oatmeal cookies

TRY THESE WONDERFUL OATMEAL COOKIES with their subtle spicy flavor. When my kids were growing up, I always tried to justify batches of homemade cookies by stealthily adding whole wheat flour and other healthy goodies without wrecking the flavor. These cookies are one of my great successes. Whole wheat pastry flour was a favorite addition because it is both light and whole grain.

1½ cups unbleached all-purpose flour
½ cup whole wheat pastry flour
1 teaspoon ground cinnamon
1 teaspoon ground allspice
¼ teaspoon ground cloves
1 teaspoon ground ginger
½ teaspoon freshly ground black pepper

¼ teaspoon salt
½ teaspoon baking powder
¾ cup (1½ sticks) unsalted butter, softened
1 teaspoon vanilla extract
¾ cup granulated sugar
¾ cup light brown sugar
2 eggs
3 cups rolled oats

Preparation Time:
20 minutes

Baking Time:
15 minutes

Makes
2
dozen
large

or

4
dozen
small
cookies

1 Preheat the oven to 375°F. Coat baking sheets with vegetable cooking spray.

2 Sift the flours with the spices, salt, and baking powder into a medium bowl.

3 Beat the butter, vanilla, sugars, egg, and egg whites together in a large bowl until well blended. Gradually stir in the flour mixture until mixed well. Add the oats. Continue to stir until the ingredients are well combined.

4 For large cookies, drop ¼ cup dough for each cookie onto the baking sheet. For smaller cookies, use 1 tablespoon per cookie. Moisten your fingers and flatten each cookie slightly.

5 Bake for 12 to 15 minutes, or until the cookies are done in the middle and slightly browned. Remove from the sheets and cool on wire racks.

plum crisp

PLUMS AND CLOVES SEEM MADE FOR EACH OTHER. Add a touch of orange and a hint of almond, and you have one outstanding variation on the simple fruit crisp. The trick is not to overdo any of these strong flavors, or you might disrupt the delicate balance. This is another dessert that can happily grace the brunch table.

2 pounds mixed plums (about 7), cut into eighths
$\frac{1}{3}$ cup brown sugar
$\frac{1}{4}$ teaspoon ground cloves

$\frac{1}{2}$ teaspoon ground cinnamon
1 tablespoon orange zest
1 teaspoon amaretto

TOPPING

$\frac{1}{4}$ cup all-purpose flour
$\frac{1}{2}$ cup rolled oats, whirled in a blender for a few seconds
$\frac{1}{3}$ cup sugar

2 tablespoons unsalted butter
1 teaspoon ground cinnamon
French vanilla yogurt or vanilla frozen yogurt or ice cream

1 Preheat the oven to 375°F. Coat a 9-inch glass pie pan with vegetable cooking spray.

2 Toss the plums with the sugar, cloves, cinnamon, orange zest, and amaretto. Pour into the pie pan and let sit while you mix the topping.

3 Mix the topping ingredients together in a small bowl with a fork until well blended. Sprinkle the topping over the plums; bake for 30 minutes, until the top is browned and the fruit tender. Serve hot, warm, or at room temperature, with the yogurt on the side.

Preparation Time:
20 minutes

Baking Time:
30 minutes

Serves

apple raisin **bread pudding** with **orange whiskey** sauce

THIS IS A CLASSIC, NEW ORLEANS-STYLE BREAD PUDDING, rich and custardy with a smooth bourbon sauce. Try making it with brioche instead of French bread. Humble bread pudding can easily become a flashy dessert when baked in individual ramekins (see box on next page).

3 tablespoons unsalted butter

2 Golden Delicious apples, cored and cut into $\frac{1}{2}$-inch slices

$\frac{3}{4}$ cup plus 1 tablespoon sugar

1 pound French bread, cut into 1-inch cubes

$1\frac{1}{4}$ cups golden raisins

4 eggs

3 cups whole milk

1 cup half-and-half

1 teaspoon vanilla extract

1 teaspoon ground cinnamon

Dash of nutmeg

Preparation Time:
15 minutes

Chilling Time:
1 hour

Baking Time:
1 hour

Serves
8

SAUCE

$\frac{1}{2}$ cup (1 stick) unsalted butter

1 cup sugar

1 egg, beaten until frothy

1 tablespoon orange zest

$\frac{1}{4}$ cup bourbon

1 Melt the butter in the microwave and pour into a shallow 2-quart ovenproof pan.

2 Arrange the apples in the melted butter and sprinkle with the 1 tablespoon sugar. Evenly distribute the bread on top and scatter 1 cup of the raisins among the bread cubes.

3 Whisk together the eggs, milk, half-and-half, the remaining $^3/_4$ cup sugar, vanilla, cinnamon, and nutmeg in a large bowl. When thoroughly mixed, pour over the bread. Push down lightly to immerse the bread in the milk mixture. Sprinkle the remaining $^1/_4$ cup raisins on top. Cover with plastic wrap and refrigerate for at least 1 hour.

4 Preheat the oven to 375°F.

5 Bake the bread pudding for 50 minutes to 1 hour, or until it is golden brown on top and the liquid is mostly, but not completely, absorbed.

6 While the bread pudding is baking, make the sauce. Melt the butter in a medium saucepan over medium heat. Add the sugar and cook for 1 minute, until the sugar dissolves. Remove from the heat and whisk a small amount into the beaten egg. Return to the pan, add the zest and bourbon, and cook for 1 minute, stirring, until the mixture thickens. Serve hot, or refrigerate and heat just before serving.

7 Cool the bread pudding on a wire rack. Serve warm or at room temperature with hot bourbon sauce. Leftover bread pudding is also wonderful served cold for breakfast.

INDIVIDUAL BREAD PUDDINGS

For individual bread puddings, divide the butter, apples, and bread among eight 8-ounce ramekins. Pour in the custard and bake for 30 minutes, or until done. Pour the hot sauce over the puddings and serve with a flair.

individual lemon pudding cakes

I LOVE LEMON PUDDING CAKE, and could easily eat the whole thing. It is light, refreshing, and yummy. Pudding cakes are old-fashioned desserts in which the cake part ends up on top in the pan and the sauce ends up on the bottom. Baking the cakes in little straight-sided ramekins is very elegant.

1/3 cup lemon juice	1/4 cup all-purpose flour
1 tablespoon lemon zest	1/4 teaspoon salt
3 eggs, separated	Confectioners' sugar
1 1/3 cups whole or low-fat milk	6 raspberries
3/4 cup granulated sugar	

Preparation Time:
15 minutes

Baking Time:
30 minutes

Serves
6

1 Preheat the oven to 350°F. Butter six 8-ounce ramekins with straight sides.

2 Whisk together the lemon juice, zest, egg yolks, and milk in a small bowl. Combine 1/2 cup of the sugar, the flour, and salt in a medium bowl. Stir the egg yolk mixture into the flour.

3 Beat the egg whites until foamy in a medium bowl. Slowly add the remaining 1/4 cup sugar and continue beating until glossy and stiff. Stir about one-quarter of the egg whites into the egg yolk mixture. Gently fold in the remaining egg whites. Divide the batter among the six ramekins. Place them in a large roasting pan, and carefully pour in enough hot water to come halfway up the outsides of the ramekins. Place the roasting pan in the oven and bake for 25 to 30 minutes, or until puffy and lightly browned on top.

4 Remove the ramekins from the hot water bath to a cooling rack. When cool, dust with confectioners' sugar and garnish each with a raspberry. Serve at room temperature or chilled.

three-chocolate chunk cookies

THESE CHOCOLATE-PACKED COOKIES ARE REALLY, REALLY GOOD. The oats and whole wheat flour in this recipe do their part to limit the guilt and add to the flavor.

1 cup (2 sticks) unsalted butter, softened
1 cup granulated sugar
1 cup light brown sugar
2 eggs
1 teaspoon vanilla extract
2 1/2 cups rolled oats
2 cups whole wheat pastry or unbleached all-purpose flour

1 teaspoon baking soda
1 teaspoon baking powder
1/2 teaspoon salt
1 cup milk chocolate chips
1 cup semisweet chocolate chips
4 ounces white chocolate, grated
1 1/2 cups walnuts, coarsely chopped

1 Preheat the oven to 375°F.

2 Cream together the butter and sugars in a large bowl. Add the eggs and vanilla.

3 Using a blender or food processor, grind the oats until fine. Sift together the oats, flour, baking soda, baking powder, and salt. Slowly add the oat mixture to the butter-sugar mixture and blend thoroughly. Add the chips, white chocolate, and walnuts; mix well.

4 Drop the batter by the tablespoonful onto ungreased baking sheets, 2 inches apart. Bake for 12 minutes, or until golden brown. Cool on wire racks. For softer cookies, remove from the oven after 10 minutes and allow to cool on the cookie sheets.

Preparation Time:
30 minutes

Baking Time:
12 minutes

Makes

4

dozen cookies

apple **walnut** cobbler

ONE OF THE ALL-TIME BEST COBBLERS! I have been making this dessert for years. I found it a magazine a zillion years ago and have been tweaking it ever since. To me it speaks of fall and crisp days spent walking through rustling leaves.

1/4 cup sugar

1/2 teaspoon ground cinnamon

1/2 cup coarsely chopped walnuts

4 large, tart apples, peeled and thinly sliced to make 4–5 cups

TOPPING

1 cup all-purpose flour

3/4 cup sugar

1 teaspoon baking powder

1/4 teaspoon salt

1 egg

2/3 cup evaporated milk

3 tablespoons unsalted butter, melted

Preparation Time:
30 minutes

Baking Time:
55 minutes

Serves

8

1 Preheat the oven to 325°F. Coat a deep-dish 9-inch pie pan with vegetable cooking spray.

2 Mix the sugar with the cinnamon and all but 1 tablespoon of the walnuts in a small bowl. Spread the apples over the bottom of the pie pan and sprinkle the cinnamon mixture over the apples.

3 To make the topping, sift the dry ingredients together into a medium bowl. Combine the egg, milk, and butter in a small bowl. Add the wet ingredients all at once to the dry ingredients and mix until smooth. Pour the batter over the apples and sprinkle with the remaining 1 tablespoon walnuts.

4 Bake for 55 minutes, or until golden brown and the apples are tender. Spoon the warm cobbler onto dessert plates and serve.

mousse au chocolat

THESE LOVELY, INTENSE LITTLE CUPS make a most satisfying ending to an elegant dinner. I was given a charming set of ceramic pots with lids which I use for this specific purpose, but demitasse cups will also work, as will any 4-ounce ramekin or cup. They are fun to serve and fabulous to eat. The dollop of whipped cream on top is a nice touch.

6 ounces bittersweet chocolate
1 tablespoon butter
2 tablespoons brewed espresso
4 eggs, separated
$\frac{1}{2}$ cup plus 1 tablespoon sugar

1 teaspoon orange zest
$\frac{1}{4}$ cup heavy cream
8 chocolate-covered
  espresso beans

1 Melt the chocolate, butter, and espresso together in a medium saucepan over very low heat for a minute or two, while stirring. Remove from the heat and set aside.

2 Beat the egg yolks with $\frac{1}{2}$ cup of the sugar for 1 to 2 minutes, until thick and pale yellow. Add the orange zest and a little of the hot chocolate mixture while stirring. Scrape all the egg yolk mixture into the saucepan and cook over low heat, stirring constantly, for about 3 minutes. The mixture will thicken slightly and get hot. Do not let it bubble.

3 Beat the egg whites in a clean bowl until foamy. Add the remaining 1 tablespoon sugar and continue beating until glossy. Stir a bit into the chocolate. Fold the rest of the whites into the chocolate. Pour into eight 4-ounce cups and chill.

4 Just before serving, whip the heavy cream and crush the espresso beans. Place a small dollop of cream on each pot and sprinkle with the espresso bean crumbs.

Prep/Cooking Time:
15 minutes

Serves

strawberry rhubarb crunch

THE LITTLE BIT OF ORANGE PERKS UP THIS OLD FAVORITE COMBINATION. I make it over and over again until rhubarb season is over. The smooth, creamy custard is heavenly on top. An alternative is to serve it with nonfat vanilla yogurt, vanilla frozen yogurt, or ice cream. But for me, it is worth it to make the custard sauce.

CUSTARD SAUCE

2 eggs
1/3 cup granulated sugar
2 cups skim milk

1/4 teaspoon salt
1 vanilla bean, split

Preparation Time:
30 minutes

Baking Time:
45 minutes

Serves

FILLING

2 cups strawberries, cut in half
4 cups rhubarb, cut into
   1-inch pieces
1 orange, peeled and cut
   into sections with membrane
   removed

1 1/2 cups honey
1/2 teaspoon ground cinnamon

TOPPING

1/2 cup whole wheat pastry flour
3/4 cup rolled oats
1/2 cup light or dark brown sugar
4 tablespoons (1/2 stick)
   unsalted butter

1 tablespoon canola oil
1/4 cup chopped toasted pecans
1 teaspoon orange zest

1 To make the custard sauce, beat the eggs and sugar together in a large saucepan. In another saucepan, heat the milk, salt, and vanilla bean until almost simmering. Slowly add the hot milk to the eggs, stirring constantly. Cook until the mixture thickens and coats a wooden spoon; strain, and chill in a glass jar in the refrigerator.

2 Preheat the oven to 375°F. Coat a 2-quart casserole with vegetable cooking spray.

3 To make the filling, toss the strawberries, rhubarb, orange, honey, and cinnamon together in a large bowl and pour into the casserole.

4 Make the topping by mixing the flour, oats, and brown sugar together in a small bowl with a fork. With a pastry blender, cut the butter and oil into the mixture until it is crumbly. Stir in the pecans and orange zest.

5 Sprinkle the topping over the strawberry rhubarb mixture and bake for 35 to 40 minutes, until the filling is bubbly and the topping is nicely browned. Cool on a wire rack and serve warm with the cold custard sauce.

TIPS FOR STORING STRAWBERRIES

- Don't remove the stems
- Don't wash ahead of time
- Rinse and hull berries just before using
- Don't store in the refrigerator
- Eat all you can when freshly picked!

super chip cookies

BACK TO BEING STEALTHY AGAIN — WELL, SORT OF. Two kinds of chocolate, rolled oats, walnuts, and a bit of that whole wheat pastry flour gives you almost everything. Throw in some raisins or cranberries and you truly have the "everything" cookie. Plus, it is really good!

$3/4$ cup ($1 1/2$ sticks) unsalted butter, softened

$3/4$ cup granulated sugar

$3/4$ cup brown sugar

2 eggs

1 teaspoon vanilla extract

$1 1/2$ cups unbleached all-purpose flour

$1/2$ cup whole wheat pastry flour

$1/2$ teaspoon salt

1 teaspoon baking powder

1 teaspoon baking soda

$2 1/2$ cups rolled oats

$1 1/2$ cups bittersweet chocolate chips

4 ounces milk chocolate, grated

$1/3$ cup chopped walnuts

Preparation Time:
30 minutes

Baking Time:
About 10 minutes

Makes

3

dozen
large
cookies

1 Preheat the oven to 375°F.

2 In the large bowl of an electric mixer, beat the butter and sugars until creamy. Add the eggs and vanilla and beat until light and fluffy.

3 Sift the flours, salt, baking powder, and baking soda into the bowl, add the oats, and beat on low until well mixed. Add the chocolate chips and grated chocolate and the nuts and mix well with a wooden spoon.

4 Drop by large spoonfuls about 2 inches apart onto ungreased baking sheets. Bake for 10 to 12 minutes, or until lightly browned on the edges. The cookies will be soft in the center until they cool.

orange sherbet with orange slices

I DISCOVERED THIS SIMPLE, ELEGANT DESSERT YEARS AGO, and it has been a mainstay ever since. If you are in a rush, canned mandarin oranges are also good, but I prefer the taste of fresh oranges.

> 3 large navel oranges
> ½ gallon orange sherbet
> 1–2 tablespoons Cointreau (optional)

1 Peel the oranges and separate the sections from the membrane. Squeeze the excess juice from the membrane over the sections and store in a covered bowl in the refrigerator until ready to use.

2 Use pretty glass dessert dishes or large wine glasses, and serve several scoops of orange sherbet in each. Spoon the orange sections and juice over the sherbet; top with a splash of Cointreau if desired.

NOTE: After peeling and removing the outer white membrane, you can separate orange sections efficiently by slicing along a sectional membrane toward the heart of the orange; shift the angle of the blade and continue slicing toward the outer edge.

NOTE: For a really quick and easy alternative, drain a large can of mandarin orange sections to pour over the sherbet and skip the navel oranges.

Preparation Time: 15 minutes

Serves

judy mac's frozen strawberry dessert

JUDY MAC AND DAVE INCLUDED US in a bunch of old friends invited to visit them in Maine one summer not long ago. Judy is a gifted cook and a relaxed and welcoming hostess. It was tempting to follow her around for a couple of days and write down everything she prepared and how she prepared it. The weekend ended with old friends perched on painted porch rockers, discussing garden plans, extra pounds, good books, and favorite recipes. Here is one we each copied before leaving Maine. It holds all the flavor of strawberry shortcake in a sinfully delicious pale pink frozen dessert. I have prepared it many times since that weekend in Maine and never without a resulting request for the recipe. Since you use frozen berries, not fresh, it is perfect all year round. You can even make and freeze it a week in advance.

Preparation Time:
40 minutes

Freezing Time:
Several hours to
overnight

Serves
8

CRUST

3/4 cup (1 1/2 sticks) unsalted butter
1/2 cup packed light brown sugar
1 cup sifted all-purpose flour
3/4 cup chopped walnuts

FILLING

2 egg whites, slightly beaten
1 cup granulated sugar
1 (16-ounce) package frozen
   strawberries, thawed

2 teaspoons lemon juice
1 pint heavy cream, whipped
   to soft peaks

Sliced fresh strawberries for
garnish (optional)

1 Preheat the oven to 350°F.

2 To make the crust, cream together the butter and brown sugar in a large bowl. Add the flour and mix until crumbly. Mix in the nuts. Spread the mixture on a baking sheet and bake for 20 minutes, stirring every 5 minutes. Let cool.

3 To make the filling, combine the egg whites, sugar, strawberries, and lemon juice in the large bowl of an electric mixer. Beat at high speed for 20 minutes (don't cheat!). Fold in whipped heavy cream.

4 Spread half of the crust mixture on the bottom of a 9- by 13-inch baking dish. Cover with the filling mixture. Spread the remaining crust mixture on top. Cover with plastic wrap and freeze until ready to serve.

5 Remove from the freezer and let sit for 30 minutes at room temperature. Cut into 8 squares and serve. If desired, garnish with sliced fresh strawberries.

WELCOME THE NEW NEIGHBORS WITH COFFEE AND DESSERT

- Drop Dead Brownies (page 198)
- White Chocolate Cranberry Cookies (page 205)
- Featherweight Cupcakes (page 210)
- Judy Mac's Frozen Strawberry Dessert
- Apple Sports Cake (page 206)
- Red and white grapes
- Freshly brewed coffee and tea

fruit sundaes

IF YOU ARE LOOKING FOR A FUN AND HEALTHY DESSERT FOR KIDS, this is it. They have lots of choices for building their own sundaes, and you have control of what they put in their tummies. It is clearly a win-win situation. Grown-ups have been known to adore these healthy mixes, too. They are great for a buffet table.

1 quart nonfat vanilla yogurt
2 cups granola cereal (see Glorious
    Granola, page 16)
A selection of any or all of the
    following, for a total of at least
    4 cups:
    2 cups pineapple chunks
        packed in juice, drained
    2 cups frozen unsweetened
        strawberries, raspberries,
        or blueberries, slightly
        thawed

2 cans mandarin oranges,
    drained
2 cups seasonal fresh fruit,
    cut into $1/2$-inch chunks
Anything else you think
    would be good

Preparation Time:
15 minutes

Serves

Place the yogurt in a large serving bowl, the granola in another bowl, and the fruits in smaller bowls. Let people create their own sundaes by starting with fruit, followed by yogurt, and topped with granola.

oatmeal date bars

THESE OATMEAL BARS WERE DEVELOPED AT WADSWORTH'S BAKERY in Princeton, New Jersey. The bakery is gone, but these delicious old-fashioned bars have remained a favorite. They work well for breakfast, lunch, or dinner. Cut them small, as they are pretty rich.

FILLING

8 ounces dates, chopped
(about 1½ cups)

1½ cups water

¾ cup granulated sugar

2 teaspoons lemon zest

CRUST

2 cups all-purpose flour

½ teaspoon salt

2½ cups rolled oats

½ cup finely chopped walnuts

¾ cup brown sugar

¾ cup (1½ sticks) unsalted butter, melted

½ cup canola oil

Preparation Time:
30 minutes

Baking Time:
30 minutes

Makes
24
small bars

1 Combine the dates, water, sugar, and lemon zest in a small saucepan. Bring to a boil; lower the heat and cook, stirring occasionally, until the mixture is thick and most of the water has been absorbed, about 15 minutes. Let cool.

2 Preheat the oven to 350°F. Coat a 9- by 13-inch pan with vegetable cooking spray.

3 To make the crust, combine the flour, salt, oats, walnuts, and brown sugar in a large bowl. Add the melted butter and oil and toss until the mixture is crumbly. Set aside 1½ cups of the crust mixture.

4 Press the remaining crust mixture into the bottom of the prepared pan. Spread the date mixture over the crust. Sprinkle the reserved crust mixture over the top of the date filling.

5 Bake for about 30 minutes, or until the top is brown. Cool in the pan on a wire rack, and cut into squares when cool.

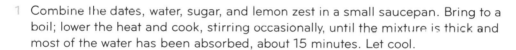

forgotten dessert meringues with fresh berries

ONE OF MY FAVORITE WAYS TO CONSUME THE SUMMER'S HARVEST of berries is in a meringue. If time and opportunity permit a few hours in a berry patch, so much the better for you, because you will end up with a truly summery dessert. Top with the yogurt sauce or, if you prefer, whip 1 cup half-and-half with a bit of sugar and cassis.

MERINGUES

4 egg whites, at room temperature
¼ teaspoon cream of tartar
   Dash of salt

¾ cup sugar
1 teaspoon vanilla extract

Preparation Time:
30 minutes

Baking and
Setting Time:
4 hours
to overnight

Serves
6

FILLING

4 cups cleaned, hulled berries:
   strawberries, raspberries,
   blueberries, or whatever
   pleases you and is available
¼ cup sugar

TOPPING

½ cup nonfat vanilla yogurt
2 tablespoons lemon juice
2 tablespoons sugar or crème
   de cassis

1 Preheat the oven to 450°F. Line a baking sheet with parchment paper.

2 To make the meringues, beat the egg whites, cream of tartar, and salt in a large bowl until frothy. Gradually add the sugar, 1 tablespoon at a time, while beating continuously. When all the sugar has been added, beat until stiff glossy peaks form. Stir in the vanilla.

3 Drop 6 large dollops of the meringue mixture onto the baking sheet. With the back of a large spoon, make a little nest in the center of each meringue. To be more elegant, use a large star tip on a pastry bag and pipe 6 disks, forming low walls around the outer edge of each disk.

4 Put the baking sheet in the oven and turn it off. Leave the meringues for at least 4 hours, up to overnight, without opening the door. Peel off the paper and store the meringues in an airtight container.

5 When ready to assemble, make the filling by mixing together the berries and sugar; let sit for a few minutes. Arrange the meringues on pretty dessert plates and fill each with $1/2$ cup or more of berries.

6 To make the topping, mix together the yogurt, lemon juice, and sugar. (This can be done ahead as long as you gently mix the ingredients together.) Spoon some topping over each meringue and serve with great pleasure.

TIP ON MERINGUES: If your egg whites are at room temperature and you use clean beaters, the volume should increase sevenfold, giving a glorious meringue. Dry days are better for making meringues, too, as too much atmospheric moisture can make them sticky.

light **lemon** bars

THIS LOWER-FAT VERSION OF A DELICIOUS TWO-LAYER BAR COOKIE is a favorite of teenagers. In fact, my eighth-grade students made these for years and never knew that they were a lighter version of the bakery favorite.

3 tablespoons granulated sugar
³/₄ cup all-purpose flour
4 tablespoons (¹/₂ stick)
    unsalted butter

TOPPING

2 egg whites, slightly beaten
1 egg, beaten
³/₄ cup granulated sugar
¹/₂ teaspoon lemon zest

3 tablespoons lemon juice
2 tablespoons all-purpose flour
¹/₄ teaspoon baking powder
    Confectioners' sugar for garnish

Preparation Time:
20 minutes

Baking Time:
40 minutes

Makes

12

squares

1 Preheat the oven to 350°F. Coat an 8- by 8- by 2-inch baking pan with vegetable cooking spray.

2 To make the crust, combine the sugar and flour in a medium bowl. Cut in the butter with a pastry blender or your fingers until the mixture resembles coarse crumbs. Pat into the bottom of the pan and bake for 15 minutes, until lightly browned.

3 Meanwhile, make the topping by whisking together the egg whites and egg in a medium bowl. Add the sugar, lemon zest, lemon juice, flour, and baking powder. Continue beating with a whisk until slightly thickened.

4 Pour the lemon mixture over the crust and bake for 25 minutes. Let cool. Sift confectioners' sugar over the top before cutting into bars.

legal blondies

THESE RICH, DELICIOUS GOLDEN BARS ARE A NEW FAVORITE. The use of whole wheat pastry flour has given them a nutritious twist, and is why we like to think of them as "legal." The inclusion of milk chocolate and brown sugar results in a delightfully sweet and subtle mixture of flavors. My granddaughter Dana and I passed the recipe back and forth until we both knew we had it just right. Dana relied on her willing band of testers to give thumbs-up or thumbs-down. This version got all thumbs pointing sky-high.

1 1/2 cups whole wheat pastry flour
1/2 teaspoon salt
1 teaspoon baking powder
1/2 cup (1 stick) unsalted butter, softened
1 cup firmly packed light or dark brown sugar

2/3 cup granulated sugar
2 eggs, at room temperature
1 teaspoon vanilla extract
3/4 cup walnut pieces
1 cup milk chocolate chips

1 Preheat the oven to 350°F. Coat a 9-inch square baking pan with vegetable cooking spray.

2 Sift together the flour, salt, and baking powder in a medium bowl and set aside.

3 Beat together the butter and sugars in a large mixing bowl at medium speed until light and fluffy. Add the eggs one at a time, beating well after adding each egg. Add the vanilla and beat until well combined. Add the flour mixture; beat on low speed until just combined. Stir in the walnuts and chocolate chips.

4 Spread the batter into the prepared pan. Bake until the surface is golden brown, the edges begin to pull away from the sides of the pan, and a toothpick inserted into the center comes out barely clean, about 35 minutes. Cool on a wire rack, then cut into 16 squares.

Preparation Time:
20 minutes

Baking Time:
35 minutes

Makes
16

vanilla frozen yogurt with fresh strawberries and hot bittersweet chocolate sauce

I CAN'T GET THROUGH STRAWBERRY SEASON without combining luscious local berries with chocolate. This sauce has been a family favorite for years, and the original version is by no means low in fat. Lately, I've been making batches that are almost as good and much kinder to the arteries.

1½ quarts strawberries
1 batch of Hot Bittersweet Sauce
(see next page for recipe)
½ gallon of your favorite vanilla
frozen yogurt or light ice cream

Preparation Time:
30 minutes

Serves

1 Just before serving, rinse and dry the strawberries and remove the tops. Cut the berries in half, but reserve 8 large perfect berries.

2 Warm up the sauce on the stove top or in the microwave.

3 Scoop the frozen yogurt into pretty glass dessert bowls. Spoon the strawberries over it and top with hot bittersweet sauce. Top each dish with a perfect berry and serve with a well-deserved flourish.

BITTERSWEET
Preparation Time: 15 minutes • Makes 1 cup

- 2 ounces unsweetened chocolate
- 1 tablespoon butter
- 1/3 cup boiling water
- 1 cup sugar
- 2 tablespoons light corn syrup
- 1 teaspoon vanilla extract

Combine the chocolate and butter over low heat in a small saucepan; stir until melted and the mixture is well blended.

Add the boiling water; stir well. Add sugar and corn syrup; raise the heat and bring to a boil. Lower the heat; let bubble gently over low heat for about 5 minutes, without stirring. (Stirring causes sugar to crystallize, giving a grainy rather than a smooth sauce.) Be careful not to burn it. Add the vanilla and remove from the heat immediately. Stir and serve.

SALSA DE CHOCOLATE
Preparation Time: 15 minutes • Makes 1 1/2 cup

- 3/4 cup evaporated skim milk
- 1/4 teaspoon ground cinnamon
- 3 tablespoons butter
- 3 ounces sweet chocolate (Mexican, if you can find it)
- 1/4 cup brown sugar
- 1/3 cup unsweetened cocoa powder

Gently heat the milk, cinnamon, and butter in a medium saucepan.

Coarsely chop the chocolate and add to the saucepan. As the chocolate melts, whisk the mixture thoroughly.

When smooth, add the sugar and then the cocoa powder, stirring well. Serve warm.

pear almond galette

THE DISTINCTIVE TASTE OF ALMONDS best balances the delicate flavor of pears when this rustic tart is made a day ahead. The rich pastry is restored to its "fresh from the oven" perfection when warmed in a 250°F oven for about 5 minutes. Bartlett pears are juicy, with a slightly sweet, buttery flavor that is prized in baking. Anjou pears are also wonderful, but don't hold up quite as well when baked.

RICH PASTRY DOUGH

1 cup unbleached all-purpose flour

1 teaspoon sugar

¼ teaspoon salt

4 tablespoons (½ stick) cold, unsalted butter, cut into small pieces

2 tablespoons lard

4–5 tablespoons ice water

Preparation Time:
35 minutes

Chilling Time:
2 hours

Baking Time:
40–50 minutes

Serves

ALMOND FILLING

¾ cup blanched almonds

⅓ cup sugar

4 tablespoons (½ stick) unsalted butter, softened

1 egg

2 tablespoons apricot jam

¼ teaspoon almond extract

3 ripe Bartlett pears

1 tablespoon sugar

1 teaspoon lemon zest

1 To make the pastry dough, stir the flour, sugar, and salt together in a medium bowl. Drop the butter in the bowl, toss to coat, and work the butter into the flour with a pastry blender until the pieces resemble tiny peas. Add the lard and continue cutting in the mixture until the texture is like bread crumbs, with some larger pieces.

2 Mix a bit of water into the mixture with a fork and continue adding water until a dough forms. Do not overmix. Wrap the dough in plastic wrap and refrigerate for 2 hours. The dough can be kept in the refrigerator for 2 days or in the freezer for up to 1 month.

3 To proceed with the galette, preheat the oven to 425°F.

4 To make the almond filling, place the almonds and sugar in the bowl of a food processor. Pulse until the almonds are finely ground. Add the butter, egg, and extract, and pulse until well blended. Set aside.

5 Toss the sliced pears with the sugar and zest and set aside.

6 Roll out the dough into a 13-inch circle on a lightly floured surface. The circle can have some rough edges. Carefully loosen the dough and lift onto a large jelly-roll pan. Spread the almond filling in the center of the dough, leaving about 2 inches around the edge. Arrange the pears on top and fold the edges of dough over the pears. The dough will ruffle and will not cover the entire filling.

7 Bake for 20 minutes, then turn the oven down to 350°F and bake for another 20 to 30 minutes, until the crust is lightly browned and the pears are soft when pierced. Remove from oven and place on a cooling rack.

8 Place the jam in a microwave-safe bowl and heat on High for 20 seconds, until it becomes liquid. Brush the pears with the jam to glaze.

dodge bars

THESE SINFULLY DELICIOUS RASPBERRY AND CURRANT BARS were inspired by American baker Jim Dodge. If you are planning a tea party, try these. I first served them on a dessert tray at a bridal shower, and they were the first items to vanish.

CRUST
$^3/_4$ cup (1$^1/_2$ sticks) unsalted butter
$^3/_4$ cup confectioners' sugar
2 cups cake flour
$^1/_2$ teaspoon salt

Preparation Time:
30 minutes

Baking Time:
55 minutes

Chilling Time:
Overnight

Makes about
18
bars

TOPPING
1 egg, at room temperature
2 egg whites
1 cup granulated sugar
4 tablespoons ($^1/_2$ stick) unsalted butter, melted and cooled
$^1/_4$ cup unsweetened applesauce

$^1/_2$ cup unsweetened shredded coconut
1 cup currants
1$^1/_3$ cups finely chopped pecans
3 tablespoons apple cider vinegar
$^1/_3$-$^1/_2$ cup seedless raspberry preserves

1 Preheat the oven to 350°F.

2 To make the crust, blend the butter and sugar together in a medium bowl until just smooth. Add the flour and salt, and mix until the dough resembles large crumbs. Press the dough evenly into the bottom of a 9- by 13-inch baking pan. Bake for 15 to 20 minutes, until lightly browned. Let cool on a wire rack.

3 To make the topping, whisk together the egg, egg whites, and sugar in a large bowl until smooth; whisk in the melted butter. Fold in the applesauce, coconut, currants, pecans, and vinegar; mix until combined.

4 Carefully spread the preserves over the top of the crust in a thin layer. Spread the topping mixture evenly over the preserves. Bake for 30 to 35 minutes, or until the top is evenly browned. Let cool to room temperature on a wire rack. Chill in the refrigerator overnight before cutting into small bars.

NOTE: Currants are actually dried Zante grapes. Do not use fresh currants.

MENU FOR A FOURTH OF JULY COOKOUT ✕

- Citrus-Grilled Tuna (page 156)
- Ratatouille (page 166)
- Chilled Couscous with Radishes and Pine Nuts (page 56)
- Fresh peaches
- Dodge Bars
- Saté Babi (page 144)
- Creamy Crunchy Potato Bake (page 184)
- Fresh Tomatoes with Herbed Caper Vinaigrette (page 60)
- Raspberry sherbet and vanilla ice cream with blueberries

DRINKS

PUNCHES AND ICED DRINKS ADD A FESTIVE TOUCH TO MANY A MEAL OR PARTY.

Beer, wine, and water are also wonderful accompaniments to meals. Though I don't drink many soft drinks, sometimes an icy glass of Coke is just perfect. Here is a selection of party drinks to add extra pizzazz to any party. Think of dipping into a steaming punch bowl of Wassail (page 244) at a holiday party, or cooling off with a tall glass of Peppermint Punch (page 246) while chatting on the deck, or sipping a Pomegranate Cocktail (page 249) anytime.

christmas **wassail**

THE DRINK WE LOVE TO HATE! Jack makes several batches of this potent punch every Christmas morning and serves it at our annual brunch. On any other day we wouldn't touch it, but on Christmas, with all the warm and wonderful smells and tastes, it is perfect! The custom of drinking a toast makes sense after partaking of this wassail. If one is lucky, one can literally drink a toast, because it is floating in the hot spiced ale along with the roasted apples. The drink itself dates back to medieval England, when the term "wassail" meant "be hale."

7 crabapples or 3 small McIntosh apples, pricked with the tines of a fork
1 quart ale
1 teaspoon freshly grated nutmeg
5 slices fresh gingerroot

2 cups dry sherry, such as fino
Zest and juice of 1 lemon
2 tablespoons sugar
3 slices bread, toasted and cut into quarters

Preparation Time:
45 minutes

Makes
1¹/₂
quarts
(about 12
servings)

1 Preheat the oven to 450°F.

2 Roast the apples for 10 to 25 minutes, depending on their size, until they are just soft. Set aside and keep warm.

3 Heat the ale in a large pot over medium heat until just below the boiling point. Stir in the spices, sherry, lemon juice, zest, and sugar. Cover and steep over low heat for 25 minutes. Do not boil.

4 Strain the wassail into a heated punch bowl and then float apples and toast on top. Ladle into punch cups and drink a toast.

strawberry party punch

LEMONADE GIVES A SUBTLE TARTNESS to this luscious rosy fruit punch. Roxanne, our seasoned Charlottesville hostess, tells us: "I have made this punch for every work Christmas party for the past twenty years, and everyone always raves about it. I have tried to get out of it, but it is always requested — and honestly, it *is* good!"

1 (16-ounce) package frozen
    strawberries, slightly thawed
1 cup crushed pineapple
1 (6-ounce) can frozen lemonade
    concentrate
3 quarts chilled ginger ale
    Ice cubes

Preparation Time:
15 minutes

Makes

4-ounce
servings

1 Combine the strawberries, pineapple, and lemonade concentrate in a food processor or blender. Cover and process until smooth. Store in the refrigerator for up to 6 hours.

2 When ready to serve, pour the mixture into a large punch bowl and gently stir in the ginger ale. Add ice cubes.

jump shot shake

WENDY'S DRIVEWAY IS THE SCENE of many small and tall basketball players trying to improve their game. They believe this quick, cool, and delicious smoothie gives them an edge.

Preparation Time:
5 minutes

Serves
2

8 ice cubes
1 banana, quartered
2 cups strawberries, blueberries,
    or peeled and sliced peaches

1 cup nonfat plain yogurt
2 tablespoons honey

Crack the ice cubes with the back of a spoon and drop in a blender. Add all the other ingredients to the blender and process until the ice cubes are thoroughly crushed and liquid is thick and foamy (about 15 seconds). Pour into chilled glasses and serve.

hot homemade cocoa

JACK IS THE "COCOA MAN" IN THE FAMILY. He produces this steaming drink on cold mornings and for cross-country skiers.

Preparation Time:
15 minutes

Serves
4

$\frac{1}{3}$ cup unsweetened cocoa powder
$\frac{1}{2}$ cup sugar
    Dash of salt
$\frac{1}{3}$ cup hot water

4 cups skim milk, or 4 cups water
    and $1\frac{1}{3}$ cups skim milk powder
1 teaspoon vanilla extract

Combine the cocoa powder, sugar, and salt in a large saucepan. Add the hot water and cook over medium heat, stirring often, for 2 minutes. Add the milk and heat through, but do not boil. Add vanilla and beat with a rotary mixer until foamy. Serve at once in mugs.

nana's iced tea

THIS SWEET ICED TEA HAS A FRESH MINTY FLAVOR and is a delicious version of the one my grandmother served during screen-porch summers long ago.

3 lemons

2 oranges

3 1/2 quarts water

12 black tea bags

1 cup chopped fresh mint leaves, plus sprigs for garnish

1 cup sugar

Ice cubes

Preparation Time:
1 hour,
mostly
unattended

Chilling Time:
Several hours
to overnight

Makes
1
gallon

1 Juice the lemons and oranges; reserve the lemon hulls. Refrigerate the juices.

2 Boil 2 quarts of the water; remove from the heat and add the tea bags, mint leaves, and lemon hulls. Steep for 30 minutes. Strain the mixture into a large pitcher and blend in the sugar. Refrigerate until thoroughly chilled.

3 When ready to serve, add the fruit juices and the remaining 1 1/2 quarts water. Pour into ice-filled glasses and garnish with mint sprigs.

cranberry sparkler

MY NIECES, GRANDDAUGHTERS, AND DAUGHTERS have been sipping and serving these forever.

Ice cubes

2 tablespoons cranberry juice

2 tablespoons orange juice

1/2 cup club soda or seltzer

Lemon slice

Preparation Time:
5 minutes

Serves
1

Place the ice in a tall glass until a third full. Add the juices and soda and stir gently with a long-handled spoon. Garnish with a slice of lemon.

fresh lemonade

AN EXCELLENT WAY TO GET THROUGH A HEAT WAVE! I keep a jar of sugar syrup in the refrigerator in steamy weather so I can quickly make a glass of this fresh lemonade.

SUGAR SYRUP
2 cups sugar
Rind of 2 lemons, cut into strips,
   white pith removed
1 cup water

LEMONADE
Ice cubes
Juice of 8 lemons (1 cup)
Fresh mint sprigs

Preparation Time:
15 minutes

Serves

1 To make the syrup, cook the sugar, lemon rind, and water in a medium saucepan over medium heat until the sugar dissolves, about 5 minutes. Remove the rind and store the syrup in a covered jar, either in the refrigerator or the cupboard.

2 To make the lemonade, fill eight tall glasses with ice; pour in 1 to 2 tablespoons syrup and 1 to 2 tablespoons lemon juice. Fill each glass with cold water and garnish with a sprig of mint.

pomegranate cocktail

ANY OCCASION WILL BE A SPECTACULAR CELEBRATION when you serve this exquisite rosy cocktail. The tang of the pomegranate is perfect with the light, fresh Prosecco, which is a dry sparkling wine made from grapes grown in the Veneto region of Italy. Pomegranates are being touted as the cure for just about anything and everything. The seeds are a lovely glossy red, and some specialty markets now carry fresh pomegranate seeds. Look for pomegranate juice in the juice aisle or fresh juice section of your supermarket.

1 (16-ounce) bottle chilled
pomegranate juice
2 (750-ml) bottles chilled
Prosecco
1/4 cup pomegranate seeds

Preparation Time:
10 minutes

Serves
10

1 Combine the juice and Prosecco in a large pitcher. Carefully stir in a tablespoon of the pomegranate seeds.

2 To serve, pour into champagne flutes and spoon a few seeds on top.

NOTE: Removing the seeds from pomegranates takes a little care, as pomegranate juice stains. A plastic cutting board is a good choice for the de-seeding. Work close to the sink, with a large bowl of cool water ready to catch the seeds. Using a sharp knife, cut partway through the fruit. Using your thumbs, pull the fruit open, holding it under the water in the bowl to minimize the splatter. Pry the seeds away from the membrane. Discard the skin and membrane and drain the seeds. Pomegranate seeds can be refrigerated in a plastic container for several days or frozen.

GIFTS OF FOOD

HERE ARE SOME SURE-FIRE GIFTS FROM THE KITCHEN THAT NOT ONLY SAY YOU CARE, BUT ARE ALSO YUMMY TO EAT.

In addition to the recipes we've provided here, you could also present some bittersweet chocolate sauce (page 237) in a pretty jar as a welcome gift. Or, when having a dinner party, pour fragrant herb vinegar into small bottles with name cards attached as part of the table setting, or make a mixture of colorful dried beans in a cellophane bag for a multi-bean soup mix, with a recipe attached. Nice packaging and ribbons show care and make a pretty presentation. I keep a box of interesting and attractive bottles and jars in my garage, which come in handy when I'm looking for a nice container for a homemade goodie. Colored cellophane is good for wrapping baked goods, as is waxed tissue paper. Pretty ribbons can add the final elegant touch.

german christmas bread

SWEET BREAD WAS NOT PART OF MY GERMAN FAMILY'S Christmas table, but a number of years ago I started making this incredibly good quick bread. I make three or four batches each season. It keeps well and makes a lovely gift.

2 1/2 cups all-purpose flour

2 teaspoons baking powder

3/4 cup sugar

1/2 teaspoon salt

1/2 teaspoon ground mace

1/8 teaspoon ground cardamom

3/4 cup ground almonds

1/2 cup (1 stick) cold unsalted butter

1 cup low-fat cottage cheese, forced through a sieve

1 egg, slightly beaten

1/2 teaspoon vanilla extract

1/4 teaspoon almond extract

2 tablespoons rum, or 1/2 teaspoon rum extract mixed with 2 1/2 tablespoons water

1/2 cup currants

1/2 cup golden raisins

1/4 cup candied lemon peel

1 tablespoon melted unsalted butter

2 tablespoons vanilla sugar (made by burying a split vanilla bean in 1 cup sugar for 2–3 days to perfume the sugar)

Preparation Time:
30 minutes

Baking Time:
45 minutes

Makes

1

loaf

1 Preheat the oven to 350°F. Line a baking sheet with parchment paper.

2 Combine the flour, baking powder, sugar, salt, mace, cardamom, and almonds in a large bowl. With a pastry blender, cut in the butter until the mixture resembles coarse crumbs.

3 Blend the cottage cheese, egg, vanilla, almond extract, rum, currants, raisins, and lemon peel in another large bowl. Stir the flour mixture into the cheese mixture until all of the ingredients are moistened. Mold the dough into a ball and knead on a floured surface about ten times. The dough will be soft and bumpy.

4 Shape or roll the dough to form an 8 ½- by 10-inch oval. Lightly crease the dough with the handle of the rolling pin, slightly off-center, and parallel to the long side. Brush the dough lightly with some of the melted butter, and fold the smaller side over the larger side to form an irregular oval loaf.

5 Bake on the prepared baking sheet for 45 minutes, or until the crust is browned and a toothpick inserted in the center comes out clean. Brush the loaf with the remaining melted butter and sprinkle with the vanilla sugar. Cool completely on a wire rack. Wrap in plastic wrap and store for several days at room temperature to ripen the flavors before serving. This bread will keep for up to 1 week at room temperature or up to 3 months frozen.

NOTE: Currants are actually dried Zante grapes. Do not use fresh currants.

MENU FOR AN EARLY BREAKFAST ON CHRISTMAS DAY

- German Christmas Bread
- Scrambled eggs
- Martha's Sticky Buns (page 268)
- Grapefruit halves
- Coffee and cocoa

cinnamon and sugar coated pecans

THESE SWEET GLAZED CRISP PECANS have a hint of cinnamon. I don't limit their preparation to the holidays, but make them regularly all year-round. They make a perfect hostess or anytime gift.

²/₃ cup sugar
1 teaspoon salt
1 teaspoon ground cinnamon

1 egg white
1 tablespoon water
1 pound pecan halves

Preparation Time:
15 minutes

Baking Time:
45 minutes

Makes
4
cups

1   Preheat the oven to 250°F. Spray a baking sheet with vegetable cooking spray.

2   Toss together the sugar, salt, and cinnamon in a medium bowl.

3   Beat the egg white and water together until frothy in a large nonreactive bowl. Toss the pecans in the egg white mixture to coat. Add the sugar mixture, one-third at a time, to the pecan mixture, tossing gently after each sugar addition, to coat the pecans.

4   Spread the coated nuts on the baking sheet and bake for 45 minutes, stirring carefully every 15 minutes. Put on wax paper to cool, separating the nuts while still hot. Store in an airtight container for up to 1 week.

crunchy nut clusters

THESE DELIGHTFUL DELICACIES are the creation of Florida cook Charlotte Balcomb Lane. I have frequently brought them as hostess gifts on weekend outings. They have enough healthy ingredients to put them in the desirable "virtuous treat" category, and they also freeze well.

2 cups whole unsalted cashews, almonds, or walnut halves, lightly toasted
$\frac{1}{2}$ cup wheat germ
1 cup golden raisins
1 cup dried apricots, chopped

$\frac{1}{2}$ cup rolled oats (quick or old-fashioned)
$\frac{1}{4}$ cup firmly packed brown sugar
$\frac{2}{3}$ cup light corn syrup
$\frac{1}{4}$ cup smooth peanut butter

Preparation Time: 20 minutes

Baking Time: 8–10 minutes

Makes

dozen clusters

1 Preheat the oven to 350°F. Coat a baking sheet with vegetable cooking spray.

2 Combine the nuts, wheat germ, raisins, apricots, and oats in a large bowl and set aside.

3 Combine the brown sugar, corn syrup, and peanut butter in a small saucepan. Bring to a boil over medium heat, stirring constantly. Immediately pour over the nut mixture, stirring until well coated. Drop the mixture by rounded tablespoonfuls onto the baking sheet.

4 Bake for 8 to 10 minutes, or until golden brown; be careful not to overbake. Cool on a wire rack. Store in an airtight container for up to 3 weeks.

fruitcake

THIS IS THE BEST FRUITCAKE I HAVE EVER EATEN. If you are one of the special breed who likes fruitcake, try this one. It is complex, moist, and delicious, and, of course, it keeps forever — well, for at least six months in the refrigerator. It's a bit of a production to make fruitcake because of all the ingredients, but the method is quite simple.

Preparation Time:
30 minutes

Baking Time:
2–3 hours

Makes

1

large
loaf

1 cup candied pineapple, diced (I buy honeyed pineapple at the health food store)
$\frac{1}{2}$ cup candied cherries, halved
3 tablespoons chopped candied citron
3 tablespoons chopped candied lemon peel
3 tablespoons chopped candied orange peel
1$\frac{1}{3}$ cups golden raisins
$\frac{2}{3}$ cup dark raisins
$\frac{1}{2}$ cup currants
$\frac{2}{3}$ cup unblanched almonds, coarsely chopped

1 cup walnuts, coarsely chopped
1$\frac{1}{2}$ cups all-purpose flour
$\frac{1}{4}$ teaspoon ground allspice
$\frac{1}{4}$ teaspoon ground cinnamon
$\frac{1}{4}$ teaspoon baking soda
3 eggs
3 tablespoons brandy
3 tablespoons applesauce
$\frac{1}{2}$ teaspoon almond extract
4 tablespoons ($\frac{1}{2}$ stick) unsalted butter, softened
$\frac{1}{2}$ cup granulated sugar
$\frac{1}{2}$ cup brown sugar

1 Preheat the oven to 275°F. Lightly grease a 9- by 5- by 3-inch loaf pan or two 1-pound coffee cans; line the bottom and sides with parchment paper and grease again.

2 Combine the pineapple, cherries, citron, lemon and orange peels, golden and dark raisins, currants, almonds, walnuts, and $\frac{1}{2}$ cup of the flour in a large bowl. Toss well to mix, and set aside.

3 Sift the remaining 1 cup flour with the allspice, cinnamon, and baking soda in a small bowl; set aside.

4 Beat the eggs in a small bowl until they are light in color. Beat in the brandy, applesauce, and almond extract, and set aside.

5 In the large bowl of an electric mixer, beat the butter and sugars at medium speed until light and fluffy Gradually add the egg mixture. At low speed, gradually beat in the flour, beating only until combined.

6 Add the fruit and nut mixture to the batter and stir with a large spatula or wooden spoon until well mixed. Pour the batter into the pan; smooth the top. Bake for 3 hours for a large single cake, or 2 hours for two coffee-can cakes, or until a skewer inserted in the center comes out clean. Cool in the pan for 30 minutes on a wire rack.

7 Remove the cake from the pan and cool completely on a wire rack. Wrap tightly in plastic wrap and store in the refrigerator until ready to serve or give as gifts. It will keep for several weeks.

NOTE: Currants are actually dried Zante grapes. Do not use fresh currants.

chocolate hazelnut biscotti

BISCOTTI, WHICH ARE HARD, SWEET BISCUITS, are as varied as the regions of Italy, where they originated. The chocolate and hazelnuts add a festive touch to this version of the twice-baked Italian specialty.

1 cup hazelnuts
½ cup (1 stick) unsalted butter, softened
¾ cup sugar
1 tablespoon orange zest
3 eggs

1 teaspoon vanilla extract
3 cups all-purpose flour
1 tablespoon baking powder
½ teaspoon salt
1 cup semisweet chocolate chips

Preparation Time:
30 minutes

Baking Time:
30 minutes

Finishing Time:
15 minutes

Makes

dozen
biscotti

1 Preheat the oven to 350°F. Spray a baking sheet with vegetable cooking spray.

2 Place the hazelnuts in an 8-inch square baking pan and bake for 18 to 20 minutes or until lightly toasted, shaking the pan occasionally. Remove from the oven, leaving the oven on. Pour the nuts onto a clean kitchen towel and, when cool, rub them with the cloth to remove most of the skins. Lift out the nuts, chop coarsely, and set aside.

3 Cream the butter, sugar, and orange zest in a large bowl until light and fluffy. Add the eggs one at a time, beating well after each addition. Stir in the vanilla.

4 Combine the flour, baking powder, and salt in a large bowl; add to the butter mixture and stir to blend thoroughly. Mix in the hazelnuts.

5 Divide the dough into thirds. Shape each third into a long roll about 1 $\frac{1}{2}$ inches in diameter. Place the rolls 2 inches apart on the baking sheet. Flatten the rolls to a $\frac{1}{2}$-inch thickness. Bake for 15 minutes.

6 Remove the rolls from the oven and cut crosswise into $\frac{3}{4}$-inch-thick slices while hot. Lay the slices, cut side down, on the baking sheet. Return to the oven and continue baking for about 15 minutes, until the biscotti look dry and are lightly browned. Transfer the biscotti to wire racks to cool.

7 Stir the chocolate in a small saucepan over very low heat until just melted. Spread the chocolate on the top and sides of one end of each cookie. When the chocolate is firm, store in an airtight container for up to 2 days, or freeze for up to 3 months.

swiss braided bread

THESE BEAUTIFUL BRAIDED LOAVES ARE DELICIOUS FRESH, and the leftovers make excellent French toast. The loaves are wonderful gifts. My children used to make this bread for Uncle Mousie, who didn't need "things," but loved this bread. Make a double batch of this on a weekend when you have some extra time, and freeze the extra loaves for use when you don't have time to bake. It is very reminiscent of challah.

1 tablespoon active dry yeast
1 cup warm water
⅓ cup skim milk powder
2 tablespoons sugar
1 teaspoon salt

2 tablespoons unsalted butter
1 egg
3 cups all-purpose flour, plus an
    additional ½ cup if needed

GLAZE
1 egg yolk, beaten and mixed with
    1 tablespoon water

Preparation Time:
30 minutes

Rising Time:
2 hours total

Baking Time:
40 minutes

Makes

large
loaves

1   Sprinkle the yeast into the warm water in a large bowl; stir until dissolved. Add the milk powder, sugar, salt, butter, and egg; mix well to break the butter into small pieces.

2   Add 2 cups of the flour and beat the mixture with a wooden spoon until smooth. Gradually add the remaining 1 cup flour and continue to stir with the wooden spoon. Remember that it is easy to add more flour as needed, but impossible to remove flour if the dough becomes too stiff.

3   Scrape the dough out of the bowl and knead on a floured counter for 5 to 10 minutes, until it is smooth and elastic. Add more flour if the dough becomes unmanageably sticky.

4 Plunk the smooth ball of dough into a large, lightly greased bowl; cover it with a damp towel and let it rise in a warm spot for 1 hour, or until double in bulk.

5 Make a fist and punch down the dough. Divide the dough in two, with one portion slightly bigger than the other. Divide the larger part into 6 equal pieces. Roll each piece into a 10- to 12-inch strand. Separate into two groups of 3 strands and make 2 braids. Repeat the process with the smaller portion of dough to make 2 slightly smaller braids. Place the smaller braids on top of the larger ones to make 2 double-decked braided loaves.

6 Coat a large baking sheet with vegetable cooking spray; arrange the loaves on the sheet, at least 6 inches apart. Cover with a towel and let the dough rise for about 1 hour.

7 Preheat the oven to 400°F.

8 Brush each loaf with the glaze. Bake the loaves for 40 to 50 minutes, or until lightly browned. Remove from the baking sheet immediately and cool on a wire rack. Store for up to 3 days at room temperature, or up to 1 month in the freezer.

focaccia with sage and rosemary

FOCACCIA IS A RUSTIC, DIMPLED BREAD only about ½-inch thick that is found all over Italy, with many different seasonings and variations. This simple version can be presented as a gift, either whole or cut into wedges.

1 tablespoon active dry yeast
1¼ cups warm (not hot) water
1 tablespoon olive oil
1 teaspoon salt
1 tablespoon plus ¼ teaspoon
    dried sage

1¼ teaspoons dried rosemary
1 tablespoon chopped sun-dried
    tomatoes
1½ cups whole wheat flour
1–1½ cups all-purpose flour
    Olive oil

Preparation Time:
30 minutes

Rising Time:
3–4 hours

Baking Time:
25 minutes

Makes

large
round
bread

1   Dissolve the yeast in the warm water in a large bowl. Stir in the olive oil, salt, 1 tablespoon of the sage, 1 teaspoon of the rosemary, and the sun-dried tomatoes. Add the whole wheat flour ½ cup at a time, beating with a whisk until well blended. Using a wooden spoon, stir in the all-purpose flour ½ cup at a time until the mixture comes together in a ball.

2   Knead on a floured surface for 10 minutes, until the dough is smooth and elastic. Form the dough into a ball and place in an oiled bowl. Cover loosely and let the dough rise for 1 to 2 hours, or until doubled in bulk.

3   Punch the dough down and knead a few times. Coat a 10-inch pie pan or 12-inch pizza pan with vegetable cooking spray; pat or roll the dough to fit in the pan. Cover the pan with a damp towel and let the dough rise for 30 minutes.

4 Poke dimples over the entire surface of the dough with your fingertips. Cover again and let rise for another 2 hours.

5 Preheat the oven to 400°F.

6 Brush the dough lightly with olive oil, sprinkle with the remaining $\frac{1}{4}$ teaspoon each sage and rosemary, and bake for 25 minutes. Mist with water a few times in the beginning of the baking period. Cool the focaccia on a wire rack. Serve warm or at room temperature. This is best eaten fresh.

BREAD BASKET

When you are thinking about what bread to serve with a meal, think creatively. Fortunately, you can now find a wonderful supply of quality American and European loaves in most supermarkets. And, even better, in many areas artisanal bakeries are producing magnificent loaves full of flavor and texture. Most of these breads are best enjoyed the day they are purchased, but can be stored in a plastic bag and frozen. We don't recommend microwaving to heat bread, as doing so tends to spoil the bread's texture.

WE LIKE COMBINING A FEW OF THE FOLLOWING IN OUR BREAD BASKETS:

- Whole wheat breadsticks
- Warm sourdough rolls
- Focaccia
- Crusty ciabatta
- Tuscan whole wheat bread
- Cheese-flavored breads

robin's biscotti

ROBIN IS A WONDERFUL CHEF whose creations have delighted diners in many restaurants in the Berkshire hills of Massachusetts. Biscotti keep well in airtight tins and make wonderful hostess gifts. They are also nice to have on hand when friends drop in for coffee or when weekend guests arrive.

6 ounces ground almonds
1½ cups unbleached all-purpose flour
1 cup sugar
1 teaspoon salt
1 teaspoon baking soda
¼ cup (½ stick) unsalted butter, softened

3 eggs, slightly beaten
1½ teaspoons vanilla extract (or other flavoring, such as anise extract)
¼ cup plus 1 tablespoon water
6 ounces chopped toasted almonds

Preparation Time:
30 minutes

Baking Time:
50 minutes

Drying Time:
1½ hours

Makes

4

dozen
biscotti

1 Preheat the oven to 375°F. Spray a baking sheet with vegetable cooking spray and lightly dust it with flour.

2 Combine the ground almonds, flour, sugar, salt, and baking soda in a large bowl.

3 Mix the butter, eggs, vanilla, and water in a small bowl. Pour the liquid ingredients into the flour mixture all at once. Mix into a sticky dough. Add the chopped almonds.

4 Thoroughly flour your hands and the work surface on which you will shape the loaves, and work quickly (as the heat from your hands makes the dough stickier). Form the dough into 2 loaves about 4 inches wide, 1½ inches

high, and 10 to 12 inches long. Place the loaves on the baking sheet. Bake for 50 minutes, or until golden brown. Remove from the oven and lower the oven temperature to 200°F.

5 Remove the loaves from the sheet and slice with a serrated knife into $1/2$-inch-thick slices. Place the slices, flat side down, on the baking sheet, and dry in the oven for about $1\frac{1}{2}$ hours. Turn them once after 45 minutes. Let cool, and store in airtight containers for several days.

almond **butter** crunch

FRIENDS USED TO GIVE US BUTTER CRUNCH AS A CHRISTMAS GIFT, and we were glad it was only once a year because we loved it so much that we had no control over how much we consumed. A candy thermometer is essential here, and a second pair of hands also helps. It is fun to make with a friend, and now I make it with my daughters.

1 cup (2 sticks) butter
1⅓ cups sugar
1 tablespoon light corn syrup
3 tablespoons water
1 cup coarsely chopped and
 toasted almonds

4 (4½-ounce) bars milk chocolate
1 cup finely chopped blanched
 almonds, toasted

Prep/Cooking Time:
1 hour

Makes enough
to share with

4–6

friends

1 Melt the butter in a large saucepan. Add the sugar, corn syrup, and water; cook, stirring frequently, until the syrup reaches the hard-crack stage, 300°F on a candy thermometer. Quickly stir in the coarsely chopped almonds.

2 Spread the mixture into a well-greased 9- by 13- by 2-inch pan or on a greased marble slab, and let cool.

3 Melt the chocolate in a saucepan over very low heat or in the microwave. Turn the cooled candy out onto a sheet of wax paper. Spread the surface with half of the melted chocolate and sprinkle with half of the finely chopped almonds. Let the chocolate set. Cover with wax paper and invert; spread the rest of the melted chocolate and chopped almonds on the other side. Chill the candy until it is firm, then break into pieces and store in an airtight container for up to 2 weeks.

cinnamon stars

THIS TRADITIONAL CHEWY COOKIE, made with egg whites and ground almonds and iced with a cinnamon meringue, comes from Germany and is popular on our Christmas table. My mother always made them at Christmastime, and I have taken up the tradition. They are my favorite Christmas cookie and well worth the effort.

1 pound finely ground unblanched almonds (about 3 cups)
1/4 teaspoon salt
1 teaspoon lemon zest

5 egg whites, at room temperature
2 cups sifted confectioners' sugar
2 teaspoons ground cinnamon

Prep/Baking Time: 1–1 1/2 hours

Makes

dozen cookies

1 Preheat the oven to 325°F. Coat baking sheets with vegetable cooking spray.

2 Mix the almonds, salt, and lemon zest in a large bowl.

3 In the large bowl of an electric mixer, beat the egg whites until soft peaks form. Continue beating, and slowly add the sugar, a small amount at a time, until stiff peaks form. Stir in the cinnamon.

4 Add about a quarter of the egg white mixture to the almonds. Stir until well mixed. The dough tends to be sticky and very fragile. (Save the rest of the meringue for step 6, below.)

5 On a wooden board dusted with confectioners' sugar, roll out a small amount of dough to 1/8-inch thick, and use a star-shaped cutter to cut out cookies. Use additional confectioners' sugar when the dough sticks. (It's a messy job, but well worth the effort!)

6 Ice each cookie with a small amount of the remaining egg white meringue. Bake for 20 minutes, or until slightly browned. Remove from the baking sheets immediately and cool on wire racks. Store in an airtight container for several weeks.

martha's sticky buns

MARTHA'S STICKY BUNS HAVE BEEN A PART OF our Christmas morning brunch for years and years. We all look forward to divvying up these marvelously sweet buttery little buns each year.

½ cup (1 stick) unsalted butter
½ cup granulated sugar
3 eggs
1 cup scalded milk, slightly cooled

1 package (¼ ounce) active dry
  yeast, dissolved in ¼ cup water
4 cups unbleached all-purpose flour
½ teaspoon salt

Preparation Time:
30 minutes

Rising Time:
Overnight

Baking Time:
20 minutes

Makes
4
dozen

TOPPING

½ cup (1 stick) unsalted butter
1 cup brown sugar

FILLING

½ cup (1 stick) unsalted butter,
  softened
1 cup brown sugar

1 cup raisins
4 teaspoons ground cinnamon

1   Beat together the butter and sugar in a large bowl until fluffy. Beat in
    the eggs. Whisk in the milk, and then the yeast mixture. Stir in the flour
    and salt. Cover with plastic wrap, place in a warm spot, and let double in
    size, about 1 hour. Pat the dough down, cover, and let rise again in the
    refrigerator overnight. (The dough is delicate and sticky, and the time in
    the refrigerator makes it easier to handle.)

2   When the dough is ready, prepare the toppings in 4 pie pans by placing
    2 tablespoons of the butter and ¼ cup of the brown sugar in each pan

and melting in the oven. Meanwhile, pat down the dough again, divide it into 4 equal pieces, and set aside, covered.

3 Stir together the filling ingredients in a medium bowl. Pat one-quarter of the dough into a 5- by 12-inch rectangle. Spread a quarter of the filling mixture on the dough. Roll the dough lengthwise, and cut crosswise into 12 equal pieces. Place the slices, cut side up and slightly touching, in a prepared pie pan. Repeat with the remaining 3 pieces of dough. Cover the buns and let them rise again for about an hour.

4 Preheat the oven to 350°F.

5 Bake for 15 to 20 minutes, or until lightly browned. Line four plates with aluminum foil. Remove the buns from the oven and carefully invert onto the prepared plates. Let cool, and then wrap up to give to friends.

FREEZE-AND-BAKE BUNS

If you don't want to bake all the buns at once, double-wrap the whole pan in plastic wrap once the buns are in the pan and freeze them for later baking. Just thaw and let them rise before baking.

metric conversion charts

Unless you have finely calibrated measuring equipment, conversions between U.S. and metric measurements will be somewhat inexact. It's important to convert the measurements for all of the ingredients in a recipe to maintain the same proportions as the original.

GENERAL FORMULA FOR METRIC CONVERSION

Ounces to grams	multiply ounces by 28.35
Grams to ounces	multiply grams by 0.035
Pounds to grams	multiply pounds by 453.5
Pounds to kilograms	multiply pounds by 0.45
Cups to liters	multiply cups by 0.24
Fahrenheit to Celsius	subtract 32 from Fahrenheit temperature, multiply by 5, then divide by 9
Celsius to Fahrenheit	multiply Celsius temperature by 9, divide by 5, then add 32

APPROXIMATE EQUIVALENTS BY VOLUME

U.S.	Metric
1 teaspoon	5 millileters
1 tablespoon	15 millileters
1/4 cup	60 milliliters
1/2 cup	120 milliliters
1 cup	230 milliliters
1 1/4 cups	300 milliliters
1 1/2 cups	360 milliliters
2 cups	460 milliliters
2 1/2 cups	600 milliliters
3 cups	700 milliliters
4 cups (1 quart)	0.95 liter
1.06 quarts	1 liter
4 quarts (1 gallon)	3.8 liters

APPROXIMATE EQUIVALENTS BY WEIGHT

U.S.	Metric		Metric	U.S.
1/4 ounce	7 grams		1 gram	0.035 ounce
1/2 ounce	14 grams		50 grams	1.75 ounces
1 ounce	28 grams		100 grams	3.5 ounces
1 1/4 ounces	35 grams		250 grams	8.75 ounces
1 1/2 ounces	40 grams		500 grams	1.1 pounds
2 1/2 ounces	70 grams		1 kilogram	2.2 pounds
4 ounces	112 grams			
5 ounces	140 grams			
8 ounces	228 grams			
10 ounces	280 grams			
15 ounces	425 grams			
16 ounces (1 pound)	454 grams			

index